FREEDOM IN JEOPARDY

The Story of the McCarthy Years

During the early 1950s, Senator Joseph R. McCarthy, demagogue and self-appointed Communist witch-hunter, dominated the headlines. Social, political and economic unrest and the spread of Communism in Europe and Asia made many Americans receptive to McCarthy's charge that internal Communism was the cause of every evil. As the hysteria mounted even honest men were afraid to dissent, and McCarthy's reckless accusations dishonored and ruined countless innocent, distinguished and honorable citizens. This is the incredible story of Joe McCarthy, who usurped judicial, legislative and executive authority, spread suspicion and terror, affected foreign policy and nearly immobilized two presidents before being defeated by his own arrogance.

BOOKS BY BURT HIRSCHFELD

AFTER THE ALAMO
  The Story of the Mexican War

A CLOUD OVER HIROSHIMA
  The Story of the Atomic Bomb

FIFTY-FIVE DAYS OF TERROR
  The Story of the Boxer Rebellion

FOUR CENTS AN ACRE
  The Story of the Louisiana Purchase

FREEDOM IN JEOPARDY
  The Story of the McCarthy Years

THE SPANISH ARMADA
  The Story of a Glorious Defeat

STAGESTRUCK
  Your Career in Theatre

A STATE IS BORN
  The Story of Israel

THE VITAL LINK
  The Story of the Suez Canal

FREEDOM IN JEOPARDY

THE STORY OF THE McCARTHY YEARS

by Burt Hirschfeld

photographs

Julian Messner
New York

Published simultaneously in the United States and Canada by
Julian Messner, a division of Simon & Schuster, Inc.,
1 West 39th Street, New York, N. Y. 10018. All rights reserved.

Copyright, ©, 1969 by Burt Hirschfeld

Credits

Quotation from Eric Hoffer, *The True Believer,* Harper & Row, Publishers, 1951, by permission of Eric Hoffer.

Quotations from Roy Cohn, *McCarthy,* by permission of The World Publishing Company and The Foley Agency, Literary Agents. Copyright, ©, 1968 by Roy Cohn. An NAL book.

Photographs from United Press International (UPI).

Printed in the United States of America

SBN 671–32189-7–Cloth Trade
SBN 671–32190-0–MCE

Library of Congress Catalog Card No. 77-87830

CONTENTS

I.	A MAN WHO . . .	7
II.	TAIL GUNNER JOE	11
III.	SUSPICION AND UNREST	19
IV.	THE DANGEROUS SEASON	27
V.	"I HAVE HERE IN MY HAND . . ."	43
VI.	TURMOIL AND CONFUSION	59
VII.	A BANDIT RAID	69
VIII.	PAYMENT, POSTCARDS AND A PICTURE	79
IX.	THE GENERAL AND THE PRESIDENT	89
X.	A SUBSTITUTE FOR VICTORY	99
XI.	THE GRAND TOUR OF COHN AND SCHINE	109
XII.	A PINK ARMY DENTIST	119
XIII.	THE PRIVATE AND THE SENATOR	127
XIV.	POINT OF ORDER	133
XV.	A STOLEN LETTER, A PRIVATE MEETING, A FORGETFUL SECRETARY	151
XVI.	NO SENSE OF DECENCY	161
XVII.	AN END OF A BEGINNING	177
BIBLIOGRAPHY		185
INDEX		187

The fanatic is perpetually incomplete and insecure. He cannot generate self-assurance out of his individual resources . . . but finds it only by clinging passionately to whatever support he happens to embrace. This passionate attachment is the essence of his blind devotion and religiosity and he sees in it the source of all virtue and strength. . . . The fanatic is not really a stickler to principles. . . .

—Eric Hoffer
The True Believer

A MAN WHO...

HE GAVE HIS NAME TO AN ERA.

He was a poor country boy out of Grand Chute Township in Wisconsin.

He quit school at fourteen to work in the cabbage and potato fields and to raise chickens for profit. At twenty, he began high school, went on to Marquette University and became a lawyer.

He grew to believe a man could do whatever he wanted to do, get any place he wanted to go, become anything he wanted to become. It was a simple matter as he saw it: learn the techniques that bring success; eliminate all opposition, all obstacles. Somehow.

He ran for district attorney as a Democrat when he was twenty-eight; he lost.

Three years later he ran for circuit judge as a Republican. This time he won.

He was Joseph Raymond McCarthy, in 1944 a captain in the

Marine Corps, and he had decided to become a United States Senator.

True, he was still a circuit judge and so prohibited by the Wisconsin constitution from running for another office. And, true also, military regulations forbade servicemen from addressing themselves publicly to political affairs. These were, to a man of Joe McCarthy's ambitions, minor barriers, easily circumvented.

Flexibility was displayed early in life by Joe McCarthy. He was born in a remote rural section outside Appleton, Wisconsin, the fifth of seven children. His father was Timothy McCarthy, a hard-working farmer who had been born in the United States of a German mother and an Irish father. Joe's mother, Bridget Tierney McCarthy, was of pure Irish stock and had been born in Ireland. Joe grew to be an awkward boy, without much physical appeal, too shy to be able to recite effectively in school. He stopped his schooling at fourteen and became a chicken farmer on land that he rented from his father. Before long, he was prospering, but when he was nineteen, trouble struck. Joe caught pneumonia and was unable to tend his fowls. The local boys whom he employed to take his place were careless, the chickens became sick and his business was wiped out.

Soon after, Joe left Grand Chute Township for Manawa, a nearby town, where he found work as manager of a grocery store. He was not quite twenty years old when he decided to resume his education, returning to high school. He completed the four-year course in one year and enrolled at Marquette University as an engineering student. He gave this up after two years and studied law instead. To support himself, he worked as a laborer, a gas-station attendant and as a dishwasher in a restaurant.

McCarthy got his first taste of politics when at age twenty-eight, running as a Democrat, he tried unsuccessfully to become district attorney. Undeterred by defeat, three years later he switched to the Republican banner and won election as a circuit judge. By then political ambitions had taken firm hold of him. His campaign slogan had been "Justice Is Truth in Action."

Then came World War II and McCarthy's entry into the Marine Corps.

McCarthy enthusiastically launched himself into the Wisconsin campaign for the Senate seat of incumbent Alexander Wiley.

His campaign literature raised more questions than it answered. One flyer proclaimed, "At the age of twenty-eight he was elected circuit judge." Actually, he had been three years older, but he sought an image of youthful precosity.

"Though automatically deferred from the draft, he left the bench and enlisted as a buck private in the Marine Corps," his campaign rhetoric said in a display of modest patriotism. In fact, he had received a direct commission as a first lieutenant.

One leaflet pointed out that he had "participated in fourteen dive-bombing missions over Japanese positions," and at other times he made more grandiose boasts of combat experience. In truth, he was a desk man, an intelligence officer who occasionally went along for the ride on minimum-danger missions, shooting at coconut trees. His official Marine Corps record lists no flying missions for him.

Reports had him being wounded during one of the "missions" —an impression he neglected to correct. His leg "wound" came during a ritual celebrating the crossing of the equator, when he fell down a ship's ladder and broke his foot.

Joe arranged for a thirty-day leave in which to actively conduct his Senatorial campaign. His energy and dedication impressed people all over the state and The Judge, as he preferred to be called in those days, accumulated almost one hundred thousand votes. But they weren't enough; he came in second to Senator Wiley.

FREEDOM IN JEOPARDY

Another man might have been discouraged. But not Joe McCarthy. It was only two years until the next election. He began plotting his campaign.

In October, 1944, with some of the hardest fighting of the war still to come in the Pacific against the Japanese, Captain McCarthy asked for a ninety-day leave in order to campaign for reelection as circuit judge. When the Marine Corps turned down his application, McCarthy demonstrated the ingenuity that would so often profit him: He resigned his commission.

Senator Joe McCarthy. There was a nice sound to it.

II

TAIL GUNNER JOE

IT WAS 7 P.M. IN WASHINGTON, D.C. ON AUGUST 14, 1945, when President Harry S. Truman went on nationwide radio to announce that a message had been received from the government of Japan signaling the end of World War II.

The killing and the destruction were over, and the United States erupted in joyful celebration. Peace marked the close of an era, the start of another.

The world had been exploded into the atomic age. It was to become a time of television and space travel, of swift advances in medical research that would extend the lives of men and make them more pleasant, of an increasing birth rate, of the demise of old empires and the coming of age of new ones, of the struggles of new nations to be born, of the preeminence of the United States. It was a time of hope. And caution. And uncertainty. And of fear.

As the war years drew to an end, life changed rapidly. Many

Americans, workers and businessmen, farmers and laborers, teachers and factory hands, people who considered themselves forward-looking, liberals, were still committed to the principles on which President Franklin Delano Roosevelt had governed—the New Deal. They worked and voted for policies that were designed to assist the deprived, seeking to bring the promise of equality to everyone. They spoke of full employment, of jobs for everyone who wanted to work, of a richer private and national life, of an end to the old barriers and prejudices, of domestic tranquillity, of social advancement, of prosperity. And of peace.

But with peace came a sharpening of domestic differences, a divergence of views that would eventually split the nation into separate warring camps.

Liberals feared native forces of conservatism and reaction, those who so often cried halt to change and progress. They warned that peace might bring reaction, even as the Administration of Warren G. Harding had followed that of Woodrow Wilson at the end of the first world war. They perceived signs of a shift toward the political right. In Texas, for example, the president of the University of Texas was dismissed because of his liberal opinions, his determination to maintain academic freedom on campus.

Yet other people applauded the firing as a step in the cause of patriotism, equating unrestricted intellectual inquiry with Communism. Some Americans continued to insist that Communists had been responsible for the New Deal, their aim to impose a dictatorship of the workingman on the country. An extension of that argument claimed that initiative would be destroyed and with it the free-enterprise system, the profit motive, business, individual freedom and inevitably the United States itself. Labor unions, social reform, academic freedom, Communism, atheism, un-Americanism—all were said to be links in this philosophy.

FREEDOM IN JEOPARDY

Those who thought this way had been shocked and made afraid by the political defeat of Winston Churchill and the Conservative Party of England by the Labour Party just before the end of the war. Here, they feared, was not only the repudiation of a national hero, but a giant forward step toward socialism. American conservatives sounded their alarm as governments around the world instituted more and more controls over national economies. Domestically there was talk of rolling back the advances of the New Deal; social security and collective bargaining by unions were labeled dangerous to the national good.

"Communism" and "Communist," these became scare words, blanketing many of the political, social and economic forces at work. Talk of political chicanery, of domestic conspiracies was heightened by real events, often exaggerated in the public mind.

The *Amerasia* case was an example. A rather obscure magazine, *Amerasia* favored the Communist cause in China against that of the nationalist government headed by Chiang Kai-shek. In June, 1945, FBI agents raided the magazine's New York office where hundreds of copies of government documents, some labeled Top Secret, were found.

Arrests were made: editor Philip Jaffe, two State Department employees, John Stewart Service and Emanuel Larsen, and a naval intelligence officer, Lieutenant Andrew Roth. Though Service, Larsen and Roth admitted having supplied copies of routine reports to Philip Jaffe, whom they considered a reputable journalist, all charges against them were dismissed. Jaffe, however, was convicted of unauthorized possession of government property. As a spy story, the *Amerasia* case proved a failure, though it continued to be a symbol of duplicity to the political right in America.

Other shocks were still to come. Early in 1946, the FBI reported to the President about information obtained from Elizabeth Bentley and Whittaker Chambers, both of whom confessed to having been members of Communist spy networks. They implicated scores of other people. One of these was Harry Dexter White, recently nominated by President Truman to become United States director of the International Monetary Fund. When, the following year, White was called before the House of Representatives Committee on Un-American Activities, he denied all the allegations against himself. Two days later White died of a heart attack. No proof that he was a traitor was ever brought forth.

The House Committee on Un-American Activities itself was a symbol of the times. Originally a special committee established in 1938 under the chairmanship of Martin Dies, Democrat of Texas, and known as the Dies Committee, it became a standing (permanent) House committee in 1945. Its mandate was "to make investigations of 1.) the extent, character and objects of un-American propaganda activities in the United States, 2.) the diffusion within the United States of subversive and un-American propaganda that is instigated from foreign countries or of a domestic origin and attacks the principles of the form of government as guaranteed by our Constitution, and 3.) all other questions in relation thereto that would aid Congress in any necessary remedial legislation."

The Un-American Activities Committee received much criticism from some members of Congress, the courts and liberal groups, it being claimed that the committee violated the civil liberties of witnesses and indulged in exposure for the sake of exposure. In the opinion of the Supreme Court, before whom many test cases arising out of the committee's hearings were argued, the committee's procedures were highly reprehensible and did violate civil liberties.

The Un-American Activities Committee (its popular designation) was most active from 1945 to 1948, during which time merely to be subpoenaed as a witness by the committee could bring the stigma of suspicion, of guilt by association, whether proved or not. In 1969 the name of the committee was changed to the Internal Security Committee.

At about this same time in 1945, Joe McCarthy, burly and black of brow, his heavy jaw perpetually shadowed by a fast-growing beard, moved around the State of Wisconsin making speeches to women's clubs, attending church socials, addressing business groups. He joined the American Legion and the Elks, telling tales of how it had been on Bougainville and Guadalcanal and other hot spots of the South Pacific.

Watching Tail Gunner Joe, as he then liked to be known, Thomas Coleman, a stately white-haired man, decided that it was time to speak to McCarthy about his obvious political ambitions. As chairman of the Wisconsin Republican Voluntary Committee, Coleman had the power to further the cause of any candidate, or end it. He told McCarthy that he liked him but that as a newcomer to Republican politics, he couldn't have a place in the Senatorial race the following year. He suggested that McCarthy apply himself, work hard, gain additional support and in that way he might one day make it to Washington.

McCarthy was unfazed, brimming with confidence. He replied brashly to the Wisconsin political leader that, when the convention was over the following year, Joe McCarthy would be the Republican-endorsed candidate for United States Senator.

Coleman ended the exchange. But he recognized in McCarthy a man to watch, a man who would go after whatever he wanted, would let nothing stand in his way. In this, Coleman was right.

McCarthy eliminated opposition one way or another. He talked one political hopeful for the Senatorial nomination out of the race, reminding the man that he had spent the war years as a civilian, that he couldn't expect to beat a veteran.

He bulled ahead, wheeling and dealing until just one other contender remained. He was Julius P. Heil, a former governor, but a man of few political skills and possessor of little self-confidence. McCarthy exploited these flaws. He had several of his supporters visit Heil at his headquarters. Each man told Heil, in strictest confidence, that he had learned that Republican Party leaders had already secretly endorsed Joe McCarthy. After listening to the same information from a dozen seemingly unrelated sources, Heil began to question his own political strength and the wisdom of making a run for the nomination. He withdrew from the campaign.

But the party powers remained unconvinced that McCarthy could win. So Joe moved against them promptly, announcing that, whether or not he was nominated, he intended to run in the primary. If this served to split the Republican vote and defeat the party—well, the political hierarchy would have only itself to blame.

Midway through the state Republican nominating convention, McCarthy learned that the Milwaukee delegation lacked a few delegates. He immediately contacted a friend in that city, telling him to get ten men to the convention, that he needed the extra votes. Where could ten sympathetic citizens be found? he was asked. Why, at the Marine Corps League, where Tail Gunner Joe was well known, Joe replied. The friend explained that many of the marine veterans were Democrats, but McCarthy had a ready answer to that: "If you ask them, they'll come—and they'll vote for me."

Come they did and vote they did, and Joe McCarthy won the nomination. Now all he had to do was to defeat the incumbent, Senator Robert M. La Follette, Jr.

McCarthy launched an aggressive campaign. He made a speech wherever there were people congregated. He shook any hand not otherwise occupied. He promised support for virtually any cause in return for a vote. And he continued to make political capital out of his military experience, never permitting facts to stand in the way of his ambition. An advertisement in the Milwaukee *Journal* read:

> Joe McCarthy was a Tail Gunner in World War II. When the war began Joe had a soft job as a Judge at Eight Grand a year. He was Exempt from military duty. He resigned his job to enlist as a Private in the Marines. He fought on Land and in the Air all through the Pacific. He and millions of other guys kept you from talking Japanese. Today Joe McCarthy is Home. He wants to serve America in the Senate. Yes, folks, Congress Needs A Tail Gunner. Now, when Washington is in confusion, when Bureaucrats are seeking to perpetuate themselves Forever upon the American way of life, America needs Fighting Men. These men who fought upon foreign soil to Save America have earned the right to Serve America in times of peace.

The McCarthy bandwagon charged from town to village to city. In an industrial district, someone reminded McCarthy that the Republican Party was generally considered to be on the side of big business. He put on a pair of soiled overalls and told his listeners how he had "worked as a foundry helper to pay my college tuition."

When it came to attacking his opponent, McCarthy pulled no punches. He managed the difficult job of suggesting that La Follette was a Communist-sympathizer and a Fascist-sympathizer at the same time. La Follette's "isolationist" position, McCarthy insisted, was proof that "Senator La Follette is playing into the hands of the Communists." Forty-eight hours later, the Wisconsin *State Journal,* a strong McCarthy supporter, declared that the cross-and-circle symbol of La Follette's old Progressive Party, then defunct, showed "the trappings of Fascism."

When La Follette, attending to his Senatorial duties in Washington, refused to respond to these or other charges, McCarthy attacked again. "We have definite information," he said in Madison, "that this smear campaign will reach a new high, or rather I should say a new low, in the last few days of this election."

McCarthy's campaign techniques were beginning to attract concern, and the *Capital Times* in Madison commented on them: "McCarthy is very adept at working both sides of the street on almost every issue. He does so by taking only the most ambiguous stands in his public pronouncements and making private calls to the advocates of both sides in a debate."

Such criticism had little effect, and McCarthy won the primary by 5,396 votes. When the campaign and primary were analyzed later, it became clear that unexpected support had given McCarthy the election. Thousands of Democrats had crossed party lines to vote for him, believing that in the election he would be easier to defeat than would La Follette. And organized labor, then heavily infiltrated in Wisconsin by Communists, supported McCarthy. The Communists opposed La Follette who, like his father, had worked quietly and effectively against them. When questioned about this strange coalition, McCarthy replied casually, "Communists have the same right to vote as anyone else, don't they?"

It was an opinion he never expressed in later years.

III

SUSPICION AND UNREST

As the Congressional election campaigns of 1946 got under way, Republicans pledged to clean "the Communists and fellow travelers out of the government." Demands were made for laws to define loyalty and provide strict criminal penalties for anyone violating them.

Strengthening the arguments of the conservatives was a mounting criticism of the Yalta Agreement between the United States and the Soviet Union, that had been concluded in February, 1945. Yalta had been an attempt to bring wartime allies closer together. But a year later some people claimed that Yalta favored the Russians too much, was in fact a sellout. When the Soviets violated the provisions of the agreement for free elections in the liberated nations of eastern Europe, the critics became increasingly agitated.

Meanwhile, at home, postwar economic conditions were improving all the time. And there was a parallel increase in personal status, especially for minority groups. Catholics were able to purchase houses in neighborhoods formerly denied them; Jews were admitted to professional schools in greater numbers; Negroes began to find employment in offices and department stores in the North.

An entire generation of young men were able to attend colleges and trade schools under the G.I. Bill of Rights, preparing themselves for richer and fuller lives. Times had changed for the better. Nevertheless an undercurrent of uneasiness rippled across America. People, remembering the Great Depression, looked around warily and asked. "How long is it going to last?"

Everybody hungered for a larger share of the American pie in those months after the surrender of Japan, and special-interest groups mustered arguments and real power to back up their demands. Organized labor stood firm in its opposition to wage controls but supported price controls. Industry propagandized for free enterprise, which to it meant continuing limitations on wages while allowing prices to soar. Business insisted that a mounting inflation did not permit wages to go up without comparable price rises. Labor held that industry profit was so considerable that it could afford to absorb increasing labor costs.

There were strikes and walkouts, sparked by the Automobile Workers versus General Motors. Then union leader John L. Lewis took 400,000 men out of the soft-coal mines. Within a month, steel mills banked their furnaces and freight loadings fell off by 75 percent. Antilabor agitation rose in Congress. Conservative Senator Harry Byrd insisted that John L. Lewis was "drunk with power." And Senator Scott Lucas added, "If this Government has not the power to outlaw strikes of this character, then this Government has no power of self-preservation."

Forty days passed before the coal strike was settled. Soon afterward the railway workers threatened a work stoppage. Were such a strike to come, it would indeed paralyze the country, stop the flow of essential goods and cause widespread hardship. Delay of shipments of meat and grain would cause starvation in Europe for the hundreds of thousands of people dependent on American food for their survival.

Aware of the consequences inherent in a nationwide railroad strike, President Truman summoned Alvanley Johnston, Grand Chief of the Brotherhood of Locomotive Engineers, and Alexander Whitney, president of the Brotherhood of Railway Trainmen, to the White House. Facing them across his desk in the Oval Room, Truman spoke bluntly.

"If you think I'm going to sit here and let you tie up this whole country, you're crazy as hell."

"We've got to go through with it, Mr. President," Whitney said. "Our men are demanding it."

Truman stood up. "All right. I'm going to give you the gun. You've got forty-eight hours . . . to reach a settlement. If you don't, I'm going to take over the railroads in the name of the government."

To prepare the nation for such an eventuality, the President went on the radio, telling the people, "The crisis of Pearl Harbor was the result of action by a foreign enemy. The crisis tonight is caused by . . . men within our own country who place their private interests above the welfare of the nation. . . .

"This emergency is so acute and the issue is so vital that I have requested the Congress to be in session tomorrow at four P.M., and I shall . . . deliver a message. . . ."

At that hour next day, Truman began addressing a joint session of Congress. A note from Clark Clifford, one of his advisers, was delivered to him. Mr. Truman broke off in midsentence and a cocky grin angled across his face. He read the note aloud: "Mr. President, agreement signed, strike over." A roar of approval echoed through the halls of Congress.

Labor unrest was only one indication that all was not well

in the nation when the fighting ended in 1945. Inflation began to wreak havoc with the value of the dollar, and the cost of living rose spectacularly. Food was expensive, especially meat, and also clothing, razor blades, women's stockings, new cars, furniture, housing. Even worse, there were general shortages. Black-market operations became commonplace, making life more difficult for the poor. At the same time, those with the most money were able to buy whatever they desired.

For a great many Americans, particularly those living in the Midwest, foreign policy was at best a necessary evil. In those circles it was held that the less frequent were the nation's contacts with alien lands the better. Isolationism, prevalent in the Midwest and elsewhere, had been quiescent during World War II. With the close of fighting, however, it experienced a resurgence. But it was no longer possible for the United States, tucked safely between two great oceans, its northern and southern borders touching neighbors friendly and unaggressive, to withdraw from the world. International responsibility, wanted or not, was being thrust upon America; her time as leader of the Western world was at hand.

This circumstance was summed up years later by Senator Robert A. Taft, the conservative Ohio Republican. "I am charged," he said, "with moving in on foreign policy; the truth is that foreign policy has moved in on me."

Nor was he alone. Senator Arthur H. Vandenberg of Michigan, for twenty years an ardent isolationist, had voted against repeal of the Neutrality Acts even as the German threat had loomed largest, had voted against the Draft Act, the Draft Act Extension and Lend-Lease. And only a month after the Nazis invaded Poland, he was able to announce that the "so-called war is nothing but about twenty-five people and propaganda."

Yet Vandenberg too would change his mind. In 1944, he

visited London, witnessed German buzz bombs falling on the city. "How," he wondered aloud, "can there be immunity or isolation when man can devise weapons like that?" Later, to the Senate, he renounced isolationism in these terms: "I do not believe that any nation hereafter can immunize itself by its own exclusive action. . . . I want a new dignity and a new authority for international law. I think American self-interest requires it."

The Senate eventually gave overwhelming support to this point of view when it ratified the United Nations charter.

In a world of nations—victors in war and vanquished alike—struggling to pull themselves out of poverty and ruin, America was rich and powerful, an object of envy and animosity. A rising anti-Americanism came into view, a shock to public officials and private citizens alike.

At the same time, Communism was on the march. In Italy, in Czechoslovakia, in France, Communism emerged as a vital and powerful force. In China, with help from the Russians, Mao Tse-tung was able to place more and more of that strife-torn land under his control. Even in South America, Communists were surfacing in local politics.

In Canada, an elaborate spy ring was uncovered, some fourteen strategically placed Canadians confessing that they had passed on to members of the Soviet embassy secrets about the atomic bomb and other military information. Even more disturbing, there was the clear implication that a similar espionage organization existed in the United States.

Fear of Communism was spreading, and there was increasing agitation to ban all Communists from Federal office. Committees in the Senate and the House of Representatives voiced their alarm. Many people were convinced that the Soviet Union, callously cruel to its own people, was brutally imperialistic abroad, that it was deliberately trying to sabotage the work of the United

Nations, that its espionage networks were entrenched everywhere, that it was forcing the world toward another East-West confrontation.

There were those in the United States who wanted that confrontation to take place at once, who were all for using atomic weaponry while the Russians were without such a military advantage, seeing war between the two opposing economic systems and political ideologies as inevitable.

It was Winston Churchill, master of the English language, who crystallized the situation in 1946 in a speech at Westminster College in Fulton, Missouri. He warned that tyranny was again on the move:

"From Stettin in the Baltic to Trieste in the Adriatic an iron curtain has descended across the Continent. . . . I do not believe that Soviet Russia desires war. What they desire is the fruits of war and the indefinite expansion of their power and doctrines. . . . From what I have seen of our Russian friends and allies during the war, I am convinced that there is nothing they admire so much as strength, and there is nothing for which they have less respect than for weakness, especially military weakness."

As if in answer to Churchill's Iron Curtain speech, Henry Wallace, former Vice President under Roosevelt and currently Secretary of Commerce in President Truman's Cabinet, delivered a contrary view. He attacked the United States policy toward the Soviet Union, insisting that America had failed to meet the Russians halfway in the search for peace. He accused the Administration of warmongering, adding, "I realize that the danger of war is much less from Communism than it is from imperialism."

This drew an angry response from Secretary of State James Byrnes, who was then negotiating with the Russians in Paris. In a message to the President he said, "If it is not completely clear in your own mind that Mr. Wallace should be asked to refrain from criticizing the foreign policy of the United States while he is a member of your Cabinet, I must ask you to accept my resignation immediately."

One week later, Henry Wallace was removed from office.

Uncertainty about the future and suspicion of political betrayals in the past combined to create a growing distrust in America. With inflation becoming worse, economic controls were emasculated and the cost of living shot skyward. Strikes and work slowdowns for higher wages to meet the soaring living costs raised tempers on all sides. There were two major race riots in the North and six lynchings below the Mason-Dixon line. On the Pacific Coast, people heaved bricks at war veterans of Japanese-American ancestry. Elsewhere, Jews were threatened and Negroes assaulted. Many people, casting around for a scapegoat for the trouble, blamed it all on the man in the White House—Harry Truman.

"Had enough?" cried the Republicans, exploiting national unrest in the Congressional election campaign the autumn of 1946. The country responded by electing a Republican-controlled Congress, the first in sixteen years. The Republican Party gained fifty-four seats in the House of Representatives and eleven seats in the Senate. One of the latter was filled by a political unknown who was destined to make a monumental impact on the District of Columbia, on the nation, on the world. His name was Joseph Raymond McCarthy.

IV

THE DANGEROUS SEASON

WITH REPUBLICANS IN CHARGE OF THE CONGRESS, IMPUGNING the loyalty of government workers, charging that the Federal structure was infested with Communists and fellow travelers, and vowing to make a clean sweep of all security risks, the politician in President Truman was moved to counter these attacks. He established the Temporary Commission on Employee Loyalty, its function to create a loyalty program that could be uniformly applied, that would protect the security of the nation and at the same time insure the legal rights of the individual. Using the report of this Temporary Commission as a basis, President Truman issued an executive order on March 21, 1947, prescribing uniform procedures for a Federal loyalty program.

The result was a vast and complicated effort that called on the FBI to make a name check on each one of more than two million Federal workers, from clerks to Cabinet officers, from mailmen to generals, from secretaries to ambassadors.

A single phrase, "reasonable grounds for belief" in the disloyalty of the accused, was the core of the program. Six categories of behavior were designated to aid a loyalty board in determining a citizen's patriotism and reliability. Three dealt with true espionage and obvious treason, another with advocacy of the overthrow of the government by violent means, already covered in law by the Hatch Act. Then there was the breach of official duties (the disclosure of confidential information, for example), and finally, association or membership in an organization listed by the Attorney General as subversive.

Public employment, the supporters of the loyalty program held, was a privilege and not a right. To many legal authorities, the loyalty program seemed a contradiction of fundamental constitutional concepts of justice and rights, placing the burden to prove innocence on the accused and denying him the right to confront his accuser.

A source of controversy during its existence, the loyalty program created fear, suspicion and intimidation throughout the government. Merely to be questioned by a security officer placed an employee under a cloud from which there seemed to be no escape. Even worse, no one knew who was providing confidential information to this board or that committee, or what private grudges motivated a fellow worker to lodge a complaint, real or imagined.

From its inception, until the middle of 1952, four million people had their loyalty checked. Tentative charges were placed against 9,077 and of these 2,961 were brought to formal hearings. Only 378 were fired, or denied employment, a percentage of .002.

In 1950, Seth B. Richardson, first chairman of the Loyalty Review Board, told a Senate committee that "not one single case or evidence directing toward a case of espionage has been disclosed in the record. Not one single syllable of evidence has been found by the FBI indicating that a particular case involves a question of espionage."

Nevertheless, the question of national security and Communists in government continued to hold center stage in the United States. There was a deepening conviction that ominous conspiracies were responsible for every difficulty, foreign and domestic, that treasonous activities were the cause of all the unrest in the world, the upward thrust of heretofore subjugated peoples, the growing might of the Soviet Union. Rather than face the very real danger that Russia presented, much of America's energy and concentration was diverted to this hunt for domestic subversion.

As the restrictions and hardships of war slowly faded into the background, the quality of life in America began to improve, and change was the order of the day. With the tempo of industrial production increasing each day, the material living standard moved sharply upward, and people grew accustomed to the idea of having extra money in their pockets; for many the first such taste had come during full-time war employment. Construction went on in all forty-eight states, and new suburbs of neat houses sprang up around factories and near metropolitan centers. Shoppers began to find the goods they wanted in stores, and it was no longer necessary to stand in line in order to buy stockings or steaks. The black market was rapidly becoming a memory. Farmers too had larger incomes and were living better than ever.

Another alteration took place in the American landscape. A former army lieutenant, once a football star at the University of California at Los Angeles, was starring as the first baseman for the Brooklyn Dodgers. His name was Jackie Robinson, and he was the first black man to play baseball in the major leagues.

Nothing remained static. The changes were swift and dramatic, not always popular. Great segments of the population were climbing higher on the economic and social ladder, demanding the rights and privileges America had always promised to everyone; new hands were reaching for the reins of power.

Old-stock Americans, generally white, Protestant, Anglo-Saxon, descended from pioneer ancestors, their existence founded on the Puritan maxims about hard work and patience, saw their dominance challenged, their values threatened, and their status as the arbiters of what was good or bad for the country coming under attack. Newer Americans, people of different customs, different religious practices, people who looked and acted and spoke differently, were forging a place for themselves, forcing those who had come earlier to accommodate them.

A growing effort was made to hold the line against change, to stand against the newcomers with their alien concepts and behavior. More and more there were calls for a return to the traditions of the past, and Senator Robert A. Taft seemed to be a spokesman for the dissatisfied Americans.

"We have got to break with the corrupting idea," he said, "that we can legislate prosperity, legislate equality, legislate opportunity. All of these good things came in the past from free Americans freely working out their destiny. . . . That is the only way they can continue to come in any genuine sense."

At another time, with meat prices rising steadily, Taft was asked for his advice on how to meet the problem. "Eat less," he said.

Senator Taft's conservatism was firmly grounded in the belief that the private sector of the country could do and would do whatever was necessary to benefit the United States. To this end, he viewed dimly a bill introduced by the freshman Senator from Wisconsin.

Newcomers to the Senate were by tradition relegated to obscurity. But that was too confining a role to suit Joe McCarthy, even after his initial effort to make himself heard in Washington had resulted in defeat. On that occasion, he had tried to bring about a relaxation of government rationing of sugar for the benefit of his friends at the Allied Molasses Company, and also those at Pepsi-Cola. McCarthy had fought for them with such energy and fervor that in the Senate cloakrooms he came to be known as the Pepsi-Cola Kid. Despite a setback brought on by opposition from members of his own party, he had made some very well-placed and wealthy contacts during the battle.

Anxious to gain some favorable personal publicity, McCarthy cast around for a device which might achieve that end. Communism seemed a likely issue.

He introduced a bill to encourage unionists to inform on any Communists in their ranks, one that would also compel employers to fire them. When opposition came, it was again from within his own party, Senator Taft scoring the proposed legislation as a danger to the Republic.

"In the first place," Taft said, "is it necessary to compel employers to fire Communists? Can we not trust the employers to do it without writing into the bill a specific clause requiring them to do it?"

Faced with such opposition, McCarthy decided it was good politics to allow the bill to lapse. But a month later he made another effort to profit from Communism. He read into the *Congressional Record* a resolution adopted by the Green Bay Diocesan Union of Holy Name Societies, which said in part:

> The Communist powers are insidiously carrying on their avowed determination to dominate the earth. . . .
> A woeful and dangerous tendency is to be seen on the part of many in high places to evade, hedge and compromise in these tragic circumstances, but we rejoice in what seems to be the determination of the new Secretary of State [George C. Marshall] to set a pattern for American diplomacy which seems to be taking the ini-

tiative in China, Korea, Japan, the Middle East and virtually throughout the world, thus putting Communism on the defensive.

The resolution caused hardly a ripple in official Washington or in the press. It was soon forgotten. And so was McCarthy's flirtation with the Communist issue. Not for years would he be able to exploit it for gain, and then it would be by attacking General Marshall.

McCarthy found other causes. He fought against public housing, incurring the gratitude of real estate interests in his native state; and he gained popularity among his German-American constituents by defending the Nazis accused of murdering American prisoners at Malmédy during World War II.

The conservatives in Congress, a coalition of southern Democrats and northern Republicans, set out to turn back the advances of the New Deal, and the result was a failure to pass civil rights legislation to aid beleaguered and deprived Negroes. However, two new laws were passed. One, a revised income-tax formula, lowered taxes disproportionately, favoring those with high incomes at the expense of those not so fortunate. And the other was the Taft-Hartley Act, designed to undercut the power of the labor unions. Congress went further. It refused to assist in the building of public housing or to extend social-security benefits or to maintain price controls or to give meaningful financial aid to public education; and steep cuts were made in money allocated for soil conservation.

Outside the country, the conflict with Russia continued. The anti-Communist government of Greece, which had been supported by Britain since the end of the war, was in trouble, as the British, hard-pressed economically, were forced to withdraw their help. Here was a very real threat to world stability. Should

Greece fall, it seemed inevitable that Turkey would follow her into the Soviet orbit. And if that occurred the entire eastern Mediterranean area would certainly do the same.

President Truman recognized this danger and moved to meet it. He hoped to shore up Greece and Turkey financially and went before the Congress to ask for the money, stressing the danger to the Western alliance, to the United States itself. The President said:

> I believe that it must be the policy of the United States to support free peoples who are resisting attempted subjugation by armed minorities or by outside pressures.
>
> I believe we must assist free peoples to work out their own destinies in their own way.
>
> I believe that our help should be primarily through economic and financial aid, which is essential to economic stability and orderly political processes.

He asked Congress for $400 million in military and economic aid for Greece and Turkey, plus military and civilian advisers to supervise the use of that assistance. This was the heart of what became known as the Truman Doctrine.

In April, 1947, Presidential adviser Bernard Baruch described what was happening in the world. "Let us not be deceived," he said, "today we are in the midst of a cold war."

And the Cold War was taking its toll. There was continuing strife in Asia, and in Europe many countries were on the edge of economic disaster, their people without suitable food or shelter, prime prey for Communist propagandists. Already the governments of Italy and France were beset by growing domestic Communist Parties.

Secretary of State George Catlett Marshall, formerly Chief

of Staff, U. S. Army, wanted to crystallize American foreign policy. To this end, he created a Policy Planning Staff (PPS), composed of specialists who were to formulate and project policy as much as twenty-five years into the future. Heading the group was George Kennan, a career foreign-service man with a hardheaded, pragmatic approach to diplomacy. Eventually the PPS concluded that when dealing with current problems, America had three choices: to make war on Russia, and so attempt to destroy the core of the Communist movement; to permit the Soviets to expand their sphere of influence without opposition; or to enact a foreign policy that would limit or even halt Russia's advances.

The last choice was clearly the most feasible. It avoided direct conflict and conceived hope in the future for a much less belligerent Soviet Union. Joseph Stalin, premier of Russia, the fount from which much Soviet belligerence sprang, was getting old, and after his death power could conceivably pass into more reasonable hands, hands less bloody and less willing to spill more blood.

More immediately, the PPS concluded that because of the corrupt and incompetent leadership of Chiang Kai-shek China must eventually fall to Mao Tse-tung and the Communists.

But of greater concern to the policy thinkers were such industrial nations as Japan and Germany, plus all of western Europe.

Out of this uncertain and dangerous situation, PPS offered a plan, a massive effort by the United States intended to restore the economic health of Europe. The nations so helped had to provide assurance that they would take the initiative in working out the details and would be able to do the job necessary to restore their countries.

Here was a break with the Truman Doctrine in that this offer of assistance represented no defensive reflex to Communism, was not aggressively intended toward the Soviet Union, was presented without ideological overtones.

"Our policy," Secretary Marshall explained, "is directed not against any country or doctrine, but against hunger, poverty, desperation and chaos. Its purpose should be the revival of a working economy . . . so as to permit the emergence of political and social conditions in which free institutions can exist. . . . Any government that is willing to assist in the task of recovery will find full cooperation, I am sure, on the part of the United States Government."

This policy became known as the Marshall Plan.

As if in reaction to the Marshall Plan, early in 1948, a coup brought Czechoslovakia behind the Iron Curtain, and Russian threats were directed at tiny Finland. Also, it was widely held that upcoming elections in Italy might take that country into the Communist camp.

Many Americans were convinced that a hot war with the Soviet Union had to come, and some said it would be a good thing. There was talk also of a so-called preventive war while the United States had the advantage of the atomic bomb. Passions ran high. The battle over the conduct of foreign affairs and domestic issues continued, pushing the country into opposing camps. And with the Presidential election in view, the Democratic Party was sharply divided, its power apparently shattered.

Southerners, traditionally Democrats, frustrated and angry at the Truman Administration because of its concern for the civil rights of Negroes, formed the Dixiecrat Party. Its candidate for the Presidency was Strom Thurmond, Governor of South Carolina.

Henry Wallace headed the new Progressive Party, in a further disintegration of Democratic Party unity.

The Republicans, confident of victory, by-passed Robert Taft and nominated Thomas Dewey of New York as their Presidential candidate.

Most Democrats saw this set of circumstances as guaranteeing the defeat of their party, unless the President could be persuaded not to stand for reelection. But Harry Truman was adamant; he would run, and what's more, he intended to win.

In thinking that, Truman stood virtually alone. Few experts, or voters, gave the man from Missouri a chance. He had antagonized too many special-interest groups: labor, big business, the political left and the political right.

Certain of victory, candidate Dewey and the Republicans conducted a pleasant, easily paced campaign, smug in their assurance that Dewey would soon ascend to the nation's highest office. The mood of the country, the perception of his advisers, the opinion polls, the editorialists—all told him he was going to win. And easily.

Dewey campaigned for six weeks; Truman stumped the country for two weeks more. Dewey remained somewhat detached, cool, aloof; Harry Truman "gave 'em hell."

None of it seemed to matter much. On election night, it was agreed early that Dewey was the victor—the poll takers had said so; the bookmakers had offered gigantic odds on it; radio commentator H. V. Kaltenborn pontificated on it; the Chicago *Tribune* called it a fact in big black headlines: DEWEY DEFEATS TRUMAN.

The experts, the prognosticators, the politicians—all were wrong. Although the decision wasn't known until the next morning, Harry Truman had been reelected. At breakfast time, the President appeared in the lobby of his Kansas City hotel, eyes moist behind his steel-rimmed glasses, his manner humble.

"I just hope," he said, "I hope so much I am worthy of the honor."

That same year, 1948, the domestic Communist issue was revived and intensified when Elizabeth Bentley and Whittaker Chambers began telling their stories publicly for the first time. Chambers named Alger Hiss as a member of the Communist apparatus to which he had belonged. The whole country was shocked. Alger Hiss was one of the bright young men of the New Deal. At forty-four, he had been in government service for fourteen years, was close to the top in the State Department. He had been an important adviser at the first United Nations conference, and in 1947 he had become President of the Carnegie Endowment for International Peace, known colloquially as the Carnegie Foundation.

Questioned by a Federal grand jury, Hiss denied Chambers' charge flatly, and brought suit for damages. Late in 1948, Hiss was indicted on two counts of perjury. His trial resulted in a hung jury. At a second trial, he was convicted of perjury and sentenced to five years in jail. Thus Alger Hiss provided a ready-made issue for Republicans, who denounced the Truman Administration for being "soft on Communism," a charge that would be echoed for years to come.

The loyalty issue was a divisive one, and battle lines were being drawn. A number of states created their own versions of the Un-American Activities Committee, and school boards and university regents instituted loyalty oaths; security checks were made on teachers and other public employees.

Individual citizens and organizations appointed themselves watchdogs over the patriotism of other citizens, questioning or accusing according to their private prejudices. The American Legion and other veterans' groups authorized themselves to decide who should teach American children, who should speak from public platforms, which texts should be used in schools, what books stocked in libraries. The repressive mood spread across the country and gave new impetus to the Ku Klux Klan in the South. In the name of anti-Communism these masked night riders sought to intimidate "Communists, race-mixers and atheists," defining them as they saw fit and meting out lynch-justice at will.

FREEDOM IN JEOPARDY

In New York in 1949, a quartet of former FBI agents published a book called *Red Channels* in which they detailed the so-called Communist or left-wing affiliations of directors, actors and others in the entertainment world.

Many people had indeed joined so-called Communist-front groups in the Depression years in their hope to improve economic and social conditions in the country, such organizations then constituting a popular protest movement. But once stigmatized as "subversive" or "left-wing," many performers and writers were never able to work again. Careers were ended, and the lives of many people innocent of wrongdoing were ruined, people who were never legally accused and tried.

While all this was going on, the FBI went about the serious business of rooting out spies. In March, 1949, agents arrested Judith Coplon, an employee of the Department of Justice, while she was delivering secret documents to a Soviet agent. That summer, too, a dozen leaders of the Communist Party were brought to trial in New York. And later, the English arrested Klaus Fuchs, a scientist who had worked on the atomic-bomb project. He confessed that he had spied for the Russians, and two of his American accomplices, David Greenglass and Harry Gold, were arrested. Fuchs' testimony eventually implicated two other Americans, Ethel and Julius Rosenberg, who were tried, found guilty and sentenced to death for treason.

All this served to intensify the threat that many Americans felt, and their antipathy toward Communism and its agents deepened and grew sharper.

To compound matters, the economy turned downward, as some had feared it would do. The Congress took countermeasures. In an effort toward economic stabilization, it revised Social Security benefits, increased the minimum wage, strengthened price supports for farmers and instituted expanded programs for soil conservation, flood control and rural electrification. Also, a broad public-housing program was passed into law. These actions kept the recession from turning into a full-blown depression, and the financial slump was first slowed, then eventually halted.

From abroad there came more bad news. In China, Chiang Kai-shek's fight against Communism had gone down to defeat. He and his followers fled the mainland, taking refuge on the island of Formosa (Taiwan). China, with its huge population, was now a Communist stronghold. Americans were stunned and frightened. They looked for explanations.

Dean Acheson, who had replaced George Marshall as Secretary of State, blamed China's fall on Chiang Kai-shek's corrupt and inefficient regime. But others in America searched for a darker answer, charging that a conspiracy had handed China over to Mao Tse-tung. They ignored the lessons of history, ignored the catalog of crimes of China's rulers against their own people, ignored the thievery and cruelty of one dynasty after another, ignored the succession of Chinese peasant revolts that had sprung up continually throughout the centuries, ignored the native desire of the Chinese to rid themselves of the yoke of oppression.

In Mao and the Communists, the people of China saw some hope for the future. Whether that hope would be fulfilled or be betrayed was something they couldn't know, but apparently they were willing to run the risk.

As if the loss of China to the Communists was not bad enough, the American public suffered another severe shock when the President announced, "We have evidence that within recent weeks an atomic explosion occurred in the U. S. S. R."

Russia, too, now owned the ultimate weapon.

Uneasiness stirred the American people. They felt beset by insoluble problems, beleaguered by secret enemies who meant to corrupt the government, undermine the military, destroy everything for which America stood. Confusion mounted, brought on as much by the changing nature of the country itself as by events abroad. Once free enterprise had been the only way in America. Now the economy was a potpourri of socialism, capitalism and welfare. Life was uneven, in a continuing state of flux. There were fewer and fewer ideas and institutions a man could cling to with any sense of security. What was happening, people wanted to know, to the good old ways? To the rules of hard work? Respect? Obedience to authority? No reassuring answers were provided.

It was a difficult time for a people who had always met problems head-on and solved them. Everything was possible in America, they had believed, if one performed according to the traditional rules. There was a right way to do things, and when things were done that way, the rewards were great. In a land where success and failure were often equated with good and evil, the increasing complexities of a modern world disturbed people, and it was becoming easier to attribute all difficulties to the cunning and conniving of conspirators, to those who would undermine the system, subvert the Republic, destroy all that was pure and righteous.

Explanations that could be readily understood were wanted, and there were those willing to provide them. Blame, they said, Communism, the New Deal, Alger Hiss, the United Nations, Franklin Roosevelt, the Jews, progressive education, Harry Truman, Negroes, labor unions, the Marshall Plan—all conspiring against the land of the free and the home of the brave.

Yale and Harvard-educated Dean Acheson seemed to epitomize all that was wrong, at least to Senator Hugh Butler of Nebraska: "I look at that fellow. I watch his smart-aleck manner and his British clothes and that New Dealism—everlasting New Dealism in everything he says and does—and I want to shout, Get out, Get out. You stand for everything that has been wrong with the United States for years."

The Chicago *Tribune* joined in, terming Acheson "another striped-pants snob," saying that he "ignores the people of Asia and betrays true Americanism to serve as a lackey of Wall Street bankers, British lords, and Communistic radicals from New York."

Adding their voices to the heightened protests at the way things were going were millions of Catholics, heretofore strong supporters of the New Deal and social reform. But now many of these first- and second-generation citizens, who aspired toward those things which Midwestern America held so dear and fought to make unchangeable, joined the struggle to maintain life as it had been.

Francis Cardinal Spellman spoke for them in a succession of speeches denouncing the Red Menace. In one he said, "The fear weighs upon me that we may fail or refuse to realize that Communists, who have put to death thousands of innocent people across the seas, are today digging deep inroads into our own nation. . . ." And at a later date his words were "This hour of dreadful, desperate need . . . Once again while Rome burns, literally and symbolically, the world continues to fiddle. The strings on the fiddle are committees, conferences, conversations, appeasements—to the tune of no action today." He went on to say that America would not be secure until "every Communist cell is removed from within our own government, our own institutions, not until every democratic country is returned to democratic leadership. . . ."

Neither the Cardinal nor others who voiced the same sentiment explained how this was to be done, short of an atomic holocaust. But what they did do was make fertile the soil of the nation for a harvest of hate and terror.

V

"I HAVE HERE IN MY HAND..."

THE JUNIOR SENATOR FROM WISCONSIN WAS TROUBLED. IT WAS January, 1950, and after four years in Washington he had failed to carve out a prominent place for himself in the Senate. He was just one of ninety-six Senators with no major legislation attached to his name, no brilliant cause to call his own; he had received no important committee assignments.

In two short years he would come up for reelection and he had no dramatic campaign issue to take to the voters. Without such an issue, he might very well be defeated, and Joe McCarthy hated to lose—at anything. Besides, he found life in Washington pleasant, in many ways rewarding. There were chic parties, sleek women, good liquor, the sense of being somebody who counted. He had to do something to keep all that. But what?

The Senator had been seeing a good deal of Charles H. Kraus, professor of political science at Georgetown University. Kraus had been making an effort to direct McCarthy's interests, suggesting books for him to read. One of these was the strongly anti-Communist *Total Power* by Father Edmund A. Walsh, regent of Georgetown's School of Foreign Service. Eventually, Kraus, along with William A. Roberts, a Washington attorney, arranged for McCarthy to meet Father Walsh.

The four men had dinner at the Colony Restaurant in Washington. Roberts, a liberal Democrat, was, like McCarthy and Kraus, a former marine and a Catholic. That night, like so many people, they found themselves attracted by McCarthy's rough charm and ingenuousness. And when he confessed that he was desperate for a campaign issue, they were inclined to help him.

Roberts made a suggestion. "How about pushing harder for the St. Lawrence Seaway?"

McCarthy shook his head. "That hasn't enough sex appeal," he told them. "No one gets excited about it." McCarthy had an instinctual knowledge of how to attract public attention, get headlines and votes. He offered a suggestion of his own. Money was something all people were interested in. Why not a pension plan in which everyone over age sixty-five would receive one hundred dollars a month? That would win votes, he was sure.

His listeners objected on two counts. First, it was economically unsound and, second, it was nakedly demagogic. It wouldn't do. McCarthy required an issue not only dramatic but useful and sound. They continued to exchange ideas.

Dinner over, the four men retired to Attorney Roberts' office in the nearby DeSales Building. For the most part, McCarthy dominated the conversation, that being his usual mode of operation. Finally Father Walsh broke in.

"How about Communism as an issue?" he asked, outlining its capacity for mischief the world over, for subversion in the United States. He detailed its growing power and the dangers it presented to democratic nations and institutions everywhere. He emphasized that people were becoming increasingly aware of the Communist threat, and he was certain it would become a primary campaign issue in the next election.

McCarthy's response was intuitive. Back in Wisconsin, even among the Irish farmers in the northern part of the state who had supported Roosevelt's New Deal, there had been deep-seated suspicion about the "aristocrats" of the East, the "radicals," the English and those diplomats in their fancy striped pants. Among his constituents, the political left had always drawn a negative response.

"The government is full of Communists," McCarthy said. "The thing to do is to hammer at them."

Attorney Roberts reminded McCarthy that people were bored with the frequently vague talk of "Reds." Any campaign against Communism, he insisted, would have to deal with specifics, be factual.

Father Walsh and Kraus agreed.

McCarthy assured them that he intended to get the facts, make them known to the public. When the evening finally wore to a close, the three men were convinced that McCarthy was going to do a much-needed job and do it well. But only a few months later, all three would repudiate him and his methods.

Soon after the dinner at the Colony, McCarthy asked the Senate Republican Campaign Committee to arrange some speaking engagements for him during the Lincoln's Birthday weekend. His subject would be "Communists in Government."

But discovering Communists to talk about was more difficult, for they avoided casual detection. Skilled agents—spies—were too clever to have their cover lifted by inexperienced searchers. As for less professional security risks, every Federal agency had put its employees through the investigatory process, and the FBI labored continuously to find subversives. A letter written in 1947 by then Secretary of State James Byrnes, in response to a query from Congressman Adolph Sabath of Illinois, made clear the security measures set in motion in the State Department:

> Pursuant to Executive Order, approximately 4,000 employees have been transferred. . . . Of those 4,000 employees, the case histories of approximately 3,000 have been subjected to a preliminary examination, as a result of which a recommendation against permanent employment has been made in 284 cases by the screening committee. . . . Of the 79 actually separated from the service, 26 were aliens and therefore under "political disability" with respect to employment in the peacetime operations of the Department. I assume that factor alone could be considered the principal basis for their separation.

Out of such readily available information, and with no firm evidence, McCarthy prepared to launch his crusade against subversion. Three weeks after Alger Hiss was convicted as a perjurer, ten days after President Truman gave approval for the development of the hydrogen bomb, less than a week after the confession of atomic spy Klaus Fuchs was made public in London, Senator Joe McCarthy flew into Wheeling, West Virginia, to deliver a speech there. Afterward, nothing would be the same for him. Or for the nation. He would become the most dominating individual in America, a power whose influence extended into all levels of government, a force felt around the world. Joe McCarthy, Communist Hunter.

Years later, Roy Cohn, legal counsel, investigator and biographer of the Senator, was able to write that McCarthy had "bought Communism in much the same way as other people purchase a new automobile. The salesman showed him the model; he looked at it with interest, examined it more closely, kicked at the tires, sat at the wheel, squiggled in the seat, asked some questions, and bought. It was just as cold as that."

In Wheeling, in the old McLure Hotel, Senator McCarthy addressed the Women's Republican Club. The members listened with no great anticipation. The balding, glowering man who faced them was a comparative unknown, hardly established in Washington. He might, for all they could tell, be another of those one-term Senators, quickly forgotten. But not after this day. Tail Gunner Joe took dead aim on target and conjured up visions of political demons and of a Holy Crusade. The ladies of Wheeling sat up straight in their seats.

"Today," he began, "we are engaged in a final, all-out battle between Communistic atheism and Christianity. The modern champions of Communism have selected this as the time. And, ladies and gentlemen, the chips are down—they are truly down. . . ."

In that stiff-upper-lip way of his, McCarthy muttered and mumbled on, reminding his listeners of Alger Hiss, John Stewart Service, Julian Wadleigh, all the names out of the Elizabeth Bentley and Whittaker Chambers testimony. The ladies of Wheeling slumped back disappointed; it was a familiar cast over whom it was difficult to become excited.

"The reason why we find ourselves in a position of impotency," McCarthy continued, "is not because our only powerful potential enemy has sent men to invade our shores, but rather because of the traitorous actions of those who have been treated so well by this nation. . . . This is glaringly true in the State Department. There the bright young men who were born with silver spoons in their mouths are the ones who have been most traitorous. . . ."

That made the Republican ladies sit up and take notice. Traitors in the State Department! The spoiled sons of the rich with no loyalty to their country! Treachery and subversion. Of course! Here was what was really wrong with America!

"And, ladies and gentlemen," McCarthy said with a kind of illogic that many people never questioned, "while I cannot take the time to name all the men in the State Department who have been named as active members of the Communist Party and members of a spy ring, I have here in my hand a list of 205—a list of names that were made known to the Secretary of State as being members of the Communist Party and who nevertheless are still working and shaping policy in the State Department."

McCarthy went on to characterize Secretary of State Acheson as a "pompous diplomat in striped pants, with a phony British accent. . . ."

His political duty to Wheeling dispatched, McCarthy hurried off to catch a plane to Denver and his next speaking engagement. Here he transformed the 205 Communists into 205 "bad security risks." And the next day, in Salt Lake City, he insisted that he knew of "57 card-carrying Communists" in the government.

When reporters asked to see the list of names, McCarthy declined, saying he would show it only to Secretary Acheson. Prior to leaving Salt Lake City, he submitted to a radio interview conducted by Dan Valentine.

"Last night," McCarthy said, "I discussed the Communists in the State Department. I stated that I had the names of 57 card-carrying members of the Communist Party. . . . Now I want to tell [Acheson] this: if he wants to call me tonight at the Utah Hotel, I will be glad to give him the names of those 57 card-carrying Communists. . . ."

Valentine pressed the point. "In other words, Senator, if Secretary of State Dean Acheson would call you at the Utah Hotel tonight in Salt Lake City, you could give him 57 names of actual card-carrying Communists in the State Department of the United States—actual card-carrying Communists?"

"Not only can, Dan, but will. . . ."

A detail McCarthy may or may not have known was that for

several years Communists had not carried membership cards, the party having taken them out of use as a protective measure.

"Well," Valentine said. "I am just a common man out here in Salt Lake City, a man who's got a family and a son and a job. You mean to say there are 57 Communists in our State Department that direct or control our State Department policy or help direct it?"

McCarthy couldn't have said it better, but he tried. "Well, Dan, I don't want to indicate there are only 57; I say I have the names of 57."

After his speech in Wheeling, the State Department had sent a wire to McCarthy, asking for the names of his 205 Communists, promising a swift investigation. Instead of supplying such a list, McCarthy claimed that he had been misquoted. Now a second request came out of the Department, and in Washington Lincoln White, a State departmental spokesman, said, "We know of no Communist member of the Department, and if we find any, they will be summarily discharged."

Excited by the furor he had stirred up, McCarthy sent a telegram to President Truman, containing his by now familiar charge. It included this allegation:

> WHILE THE RECORDS ARE NOT AVAILABLE TO ME I KNOW ABSOLUTELY OF ONE GROUP OF APPROXIMATELY THREE HUNDRED CERTIFIED TO THE SECRETARY FOR DISCHARGE BECAUSE OF COMMUNISM. HE ACTUALLY DISCHARGED APPROXIMATELY EIGHTY.

And it also claimed:

> DESPITE THIS STATE DEPARTMENT BLACKOUT, WE HAVE BEEN ABLE TO COMPILE A LIST OF 57 COMMUNISTS IN THE STATE DEPARTMENT.

William F. Buckley, Jr., longtime supporter of Senator McCarthy and one of the intellectual leaders of the conservative movement in the United States, wrote of this that "McCarthy . . . could never hope to prove that specific charge. . . ."

In Reno, Nevada, McCarthy alleged, "In my opinion the State Department, which is one of the most important government departments, is thoroughly infested with Communists. I have in my hand 57 cases of individuals who would appear to be either card-carrying members or certainly loyal to the Communist Party but who nevertheless are still helping to shape our foreign policy."

At still another time and place, he spoke about "81 known Communist agents in the State Department," people whose names he refused to divulge. Building a case for an insidious alien-directed conspiracy, he accused President Truman of being "a prisoner of a bunch of twisted intellectuals telling only what they want him to know."

205. 81. 57. Whatever the number, Joe McCarthy had obviously found the political issue he wanted. He raised the ghost of dark conspiracy, of traitors at the highest levels, of British perfidy, of the effete easterners, of Harvard, of security risks, of an intellectual plot to capture the mind of President Harry Truman. Black headlines splashed all across the country, and as quickly as that Senator Joe McCarthy had captured national attention, become a crusader on a sacred and patriotic mission.

That McCarthy was saying nothing new was known to many informed people. It had all been said before by other Communist-hunters such as Congressmen Richard Nixon, Parnell Thomas and William Jenner. But McCarthy possessed some intangible quality that made people in all walks of life respond to him, support his cause, urge him on. A product of his time, he shaped the time. The McCarthy era had been spectacularly launched. It was impossible to ignore McCarthy. The President issued an angry denial. Dean Acheson refuted the Senator's figures. And the Senate, a body profoundly concerned with national security, demanded that he explain his charges.

On February 20, McCarthy strode onto the Senate floor, briefcase in hand overflowing with papers and official-looking documents. The moment to address his colleagues had come. He stood next to his desk on the Republican side of the aisle, looking properly somber.

"I wish to discuss a subject tonight which concerns me," he began. He went on to say that he had pierced "Truman's iron curtain of secrecy," and had come up with 81 security cases which he intended to present, but which he did not identify.

Senator Scott Lucas, the Majority Leader, asked the junior Senator from Wisconsin to connect his 81 cases with the earlier mentioned 205 names and the 57 names.

"I do not believe," McCarthy replied, with no special emphasis, "I mentioned the figure 205. I believe I said over 200. . . . I am only giving the Senate cases in which it is clear there is a definite Communist connection . . . persons whom I consider to be Communists in the State Department." Then, softening the accusation, he added, "I may say that I know that some of these individuals whose cases I am giving the Senate are no longer in the State Department. A sizable number of them are not." As a matter of fact, he commented, some of them were not even Communists.

Confusion settled over the listening Senators as McCarthy went into detail. Cases 1 and 2, it seemed, plus a few others, didn't actually work for the State Department, but for the United Nations; and case 3 turned out to be the same as case 4; also case 9 and case 77. Case 14 turned up within the framework of case 41 and proved to be a person so violently *anti-*Communist that the Secretary had been compelled to discharge him. Cases 13 and 78 were merely applicants for jobs. Case 52 was accused of nothing but had worked for case number 16 who, McCarthy insisted, was according to "State Department files . . . one of the most dangerous espionage agents in the Department." Case 12 had once labored in the Department of Commerce—McCarthy was unable to locate him. Case 62, the Senator confessed, was "not important insofar as Communistic activities are concerned." Of case 40, McCarthy said that he did "not have much information on this except the general statement of the agency that there is nothing in the files to disprove his Communist connections." McCarthy managed to avoid mention of cases 15, 27, 37 and 59. Cases 21 through 26 were identified as having worked for Voice of America, with nothing more incriminating against them than that.

To display his objectivity, McCarthy directed attention to case 72 which was "the direct opposite of the cases I have been reading. I do not confuse this man as being a Communist. This individual was very highly recommended by several witnesses as a high type of man, a democratic American who . . . opposes communism."

Eventually it was revealed that the dossiers McCarthy had been referring to were the files which the State Department itself had supplied to the House of Representatives Appropriations Committee. He was in fact using the 57 cases which the Department admitted were then in its employ, fleshing out the list with the names of persons who had resigned or been fired prior to 1948.

When asked about the different sets of figures he had been quoting, McCarthy responded with heat. "Let's stop this silly numbers game."

Others agreed. But for different reasons.

The Majority Leader wanted to know if the published reports of McCarthy's Wheeling speech were accurate. He was rebuffed.

"I may say," McCarthy told him, "if the Senator is going to make a farce of this, I will not yield to him. I shall not answer any more silly questions of the Senator. This is too important, too serious a matter for that."

Senator Herbert H. Lehman of New York considered the matter serious enough to ask McCarthy to be more specific, to be more precise in his language.

"I am afraid," was the answer he received, "that if it is not clear to the Senator now, I shall never be able to make it clear to him, no matter how much further explanation I make."

Here was a taste of things to come. McCarthy plowing straight ahead, ignoring questions he chose to ignore, scorning forthright explanations, disregarding accepted procedures, disregarding due process as guaranteed in the Constitution, assuming a cavalier attitude toward anyone who failed to support him. He had found his game, ran it according to his own rules, changing the rules as it suited him to change them, skillful enough to raise doubts and sow confusion. Reason, logic, honesty, courtesy—all of these were eliminated from the McCarthy rules.

"I urge," McCarthy told his colleagues, "that the proper Senate committee convene, and I shall be glad to give the committee the names. . . . I should like to assure . . . that I will not say anything on the Senate floor which I will not say off the floor. On the day when I take advantage of the security we have on the Senate floor, on that day I will resign from the Senate."

That statement alone gained McCarthy many supporters. Clearly he was not afraid to risk lawsuits, which was translated by many people to mean that he must have evidence to back up his accusations. But they were to have a long wait before the Senator made any specific charges without Senatorial immunity.

Anxious to separate fact from fancy, the Senate assigned a subcommittee of the Foreign Relations Committee to investigate McCarthy's allegations. Millard Tydings, a conservative Democrat of Maryland and long an opponent of the New Deal and its progressive legislation, was named chairman. A distinguished-looking man, gray-haired, with a patrician bearing, Tydings held a deep respect for the authority and dignity of the legislative body he served and was equally respected by it.

On March 8, at ten o'clock in the morning, the subcommittee was called into session. Spectators crowded into the marble walled and columned Caucus Room of the Old Senate Building as the five Senators comprising the investigatory subcommittee took their places along one side of the wide committee table. Behind them, along the wall, was a group of other concerned Senators and staff members. A small army of reporters and columnists sat at the press tables. And there, complete with bulging briefcase and a solitary assistant, was Senator Joe McCarthy. The stage was set.

The hearings lasted for four months, muddling the situation as McCarthy demonstrated his talent for obscuring facts. He issued half-truths and innuendoes. He refused to supply the names of persons he said he intended to accuse in public session. And in this, and other matters, he received support from fellow Republican Senators Bourke Hickenlooper and Henry Cabot Lodge.

The McCarthy technique was obvious but effective. He would begin with a series of allegations against someone, making repeated references to Civil Service files, alluding to the Loyalty Commission, suggesting information that had supposedly come out of the confidential files of the FBI. He made no effort to substantiate any charges, heaped the burden of proof on his listeners.

"This committee," he would say, "can very well determine where the truth lies by saying, 'We shall get those files.' When you get those files, then you will know whether every word I have spoken here is true."

Thus he blatantly placed the burden of proof onto the "court" and off the shoulders of the "prosecutor." As a tactic for gathering widespread public support, it worked, and people rallied to his side. It was, however, a device that would have been tolerated in no court of law, for American jurisprudence protects the accused from loose charges. Yet, under the blurred rules of a Congressional committee, it was a telling strategy. The result was chaos.

McCarthy began his performance before the subcommittee by naming Judge Dorothy Kenyon, a lady who had never worked for the State Department. In 1947, she had been appointed to the United Nations Commission on the Status of Women. A dedicated worker for the public good, Judge Kenyon had joined organizations with more enthusiasm than discretion. Some of them turned out to be Communist fronts, and she left them quickly. But McCarthy stressed that for ten years she had been connected "with at least twenty-eight Communist-front organizations." He neglected to mention that she had resigned from most of them.

"I think that it is important," he continued, "to know that the statement I shall make here today . . . is based on documented evidence, and these documents I will present to the committee as I go along."

The documents turned out to be letterheads, petitions and sponsor lists for meetings or dinners for a variety of diverse causes. He also used unsupported allegations made before the House Committee on Un-American Activities and the California Un-American Activities Committee, before which Judge Kenyon's name had been mentioned.

"For the guidance of the committee," McCarthy said, "I hand you herewith exhibit number two [a printed letterhead], which fully documents Miss Kenyon's affiliation with the National Council of American-Soviet Friendship. On November sixteenth, 1948, Miss Kenyon, as a member of the board of sponsors of this officially declared subversive organization, welcomed the Red

Dean of Canterbury, Hewlett Johnson, at a rally in Madison Square Garden in the City of New York."

Senator Brien McMahon of Connecticut broke in. "Just a minute, Senator. The National Council of American-Soviet Friendship had quite a vogue when we were cobelligerents back during the war days. I think there are a couple of Senators in the United States who are still members."

"The Senator is talking about war days," McCarthy shot back. "This document is dated late 1948. In this case, it was declared subversive by the House Un-American Activities Committee, the California Un-American Activities Committee and the Attorney General."

"Senator McCarthy," Chairman Tydings said, "I see some names here which I think it only fair ought to be associated with the evidence you have given. I see such names as Ernest Hemingway, Dr. Harold Urey . . . the Honorable Stanley Isaacs. . . ." Tydings read into the record some fifty additional names on the letterhead, some of the foremost people in the country and from all walks of life.

So it went. McCarthy naming names, insisting it was the committee's duty to obtain government files, demanding action, soiling reputations, forcing citizens to defend themselves against vague suggestions of wrongdoing.

Whether in front of the committee, or on the floor of the Senate, McCarthy utilized the press of the nation for his own ends. If reporters failed to come to him for a story, he went after them, favoring those sympathetic to him with suggestions of revelations still to come. Soon too it became evident that he had erected a personal intelligence apparatus throughout official Washington, persons working in the bureaucracy who were supplying him with information from confidential files, in violation of Federal regulations.

Senator Tydings tried to point out the limits of the subcommittee's authority. "You have left the committee in a rather embarrassing position," he told McCarthy. "How do we get the records? We are authorized to get them . . . if you or somebody makes a specific charge."

"I am not making charges," McCarthy insisted. "I am giving the committee information of individuals who appear by all the rules of common sense as being very bad security risks. . . . I am not in a position to file any formal charges. . . . If you want me to charge from the evidence . . ."

What evidence? people were asking. Nothing remotely approaching evidence had been presented.

A sincere man, dedicated to doing a proper job, Tydings decided to act. He asked President Truman to allow the committee to study the restricted files, and the President agreed.

McCarthy responded at once, labeling the move "a phony offer of phony files," insisting that they had been "raped and rifled." Those who agreed with him nodded knowingly; the conspiracy was doing its ominous work.

To ascertain the truth, J. Edgar Hoover, director of the FBI, was asked to investigate. He assured the committee chairman that "the State Department files were intact."

That barely slowed Joe McCarthy. He charged off in another direction. He would name, he announced, the man who had been Alger Hiss's superior "in the espionage ring in the State Department." He intended, he vowed, to "stand or fall on this one. If I am shown to be wrong on this, I think the subcommittee would be justified in not taking my other cases too seriously." The man whom he was going to name, McCarthy declared solemnly, was "the top Russian espionage agent" in the United States.

The nation braced for the impact.

VI

TURMOIL AND CONFUSION

OWEN J. LATTIMORE WAS SENATOR MCCARTHY'S SOVIET SPY chief.

Lattimore was forty-nine years old and married, a slender man, intense, a professor of political science at Johns Hopkins University. He had spent a great deal of time in Mongolia and China, had served during World War II as political adviser to Chiang Kai-shek, had authored a number of books about the Orient. He had been chief of Pacific operations for the Office of War Information, had traveled through Soviet Siberia and China with Vice President Henry Wallace in 1944, was economic adviser on the President's Reparation Mission to Japan in 1946, a participant in a State Department conference on China policy in 1949. In the years before the war, Lattimore had played an important role in the Institute for Pacific Relations. It was this attachment that projected Lattimore's name into the security stream and brought him to McCarthy's attention. Though he had never worked for it, the State Department had occasionally consulted Lattimore on various matters.

Lattimore was in Afghanistan with the United Nations Technical Assistance Mission when a telegram arrived from the Associated Press informing him of McCarthy's accusation and asking for a reply. Lattimore responded:

MCCARTHY'S OFF RECORD RANTINGS PURE MOONSHINE STOP DELIGHTED HIS WHOLE CASE RESTS ON ME AS THIS MEANS HE WILL FALL FLAT ON FACE STOP EXACTLY WHAT HE HAS SAID ON RECORD UNKNOWN HERE SO CANNOT REPLY IN DETAIL BUT WILL BE HOME IN FEW DAYS AND WILL CONTACT YOU THEN STOP

To the State Department, to the President, to others in the Federal structure to whom McCarthy's unsubstantiated attacks were causing problems and the disruption of normal operations, the Lattimore situation offered a chance to strike back. Lattimore was ordered to return from Afghanistan, and McCarthy was invited to place his case against him before the Tydings committee.

But McCarthy wasn't anxious for such a confrontation. The burden of proof, he insisted, lay with the committee. It was its responsibility to prove his charges. Inspect the records of the loyalty boards. Look into FBI files. That's where the evidence rested, he told the committee.

But the policy of the FBI was to keep its files inviolate. There was no reason, however, why Bureau Director J. Edgar Hoover could not study the file in question and report his findings to Congress.

Hoover appeared before the committee. He warned that, should the FBI be made to open its files, it would bring about the alienation of its sources of information as well as the "complete collapse" of departmental procedures. He pointed out that FBI dossiers contained gossip, unchecked rumor, a catalog of fact and fancy, accurate and inaccurate data. As for Owen Lattimore's file, Hoover said that he had studied it personally and that it contained no proof that would uphold the McCarthy charge. He also presented to the committee a summary of all FBI-acquired knowledge about Lattimore.

Hoover's emphatic statement denying McCarthy's allegations about Lattimore didn't stop McCarthy. He insisted that he had information about Lattimore which the FBI chief did not. Few people were willing to accept that, and McCarthy began to back off from his earlier position. "In the case of Lattimore," he conceded, "I may have placed too much stress on whether or not he had been an espionage agent." Not that it mattered, McCarthy added, suggesting that Lattimore was the "chief architect of our Far Eastern policy . . . forgetting for the time being any question of membership in the Communist Party or participation in espionage."

Other witnesses were summoned. There was Louis Budenz, former editor of the Communist *Daily Worker*. He said that he had been "officially informed" that Owen Lattimore was a member of the party underground. But Budenz, who had been an FBI informer for many years, admitted that he had never mentioned Lattimore's name to the bureau.

Dr. Bella Dodd, once a top Communist, had left the party, converted to Catholicism. She addressed herself to the question of Owen Lattimore. "In all my association with the Communist Party, I never heard his name mentioned either as a party member or as a fellow traveler or even as a friend."

Earl Browder, former head of the American Communist Party, said he had never heard Lattimore's name mentioned in party circles, did not know him to be a member.

The next witness was Frederick Vanderbilt Field, a financial contributor to the party, who testified that he knew Lattimore but not as a Communist.

Freda Utley, a writer and ex-Communist, claimed to have no proof that Lattimore was a Communist but said she suspected that he followed the party line.

Brigadier General Elliot Thorpe, chief of counter-espionage and civil intelligence for General Douglas MacArthur during the war, had been involved in investigations of Lattimore on three separate occasions. He said the result of these inquiries was that Lattimore was considered loyal enough to be allowed access to top-secret material. General Thorpe pointed out that Lattimore supported the Marshall Plan, which Russia opposed, and had helped raise funds for Finland when that country came under Soviet military attack.

The hearings went on, and McCarthy continued to dominate the headlines. He found support in a variety of places. Senator Taft, who had earlier referred to McCarthy's Wheeling speech as "a perfectly reckless performance," now changed his tune. He advised the junior Senator, if one case didn't work, to try another. Mr. Republican, as Taft was known, wanted to hurt the Democrats and the Truman Administration in order to assure victory for his party in the next election.

Eugene Lyons, a veteran anti-Communist writer, had viewed McCarthyism as a danger, warning that "the hooting and whistling of the press and on the air should not be permitted to drown out the facts. . . ." Yet he also subsequently spoke for McCarthy.

Nor was he alone. An Army fell in behind McCarthy, an assemblage of honest anti-Communists and of malcontents, of frightened people and of persons with private axes to grind, of extremists who found in the undisciplined Senator a kindred soul.

Money began coming in from contributors small and large. Many were motivated by sincerity, dedicated to the welfare of the country and hopeful of eliminating subversives from national life. Others had personal aims in view, profitable endeavors to protect.

There was, for example, Alfred Kohlberg, an importer of lace from Nationalist China, where it was produced cheaply by poor peasant labor, and sold in the United States at considerable profit. A veteran lobbyist for Chiang Kai-shek, Kohlberg had published the following attack on Professor Philip Caryl Jessup in *China Monthly* in August, 1949:

> Professor Jessup must therefore be honored by our State Department as the initiator of the smear campaign against Nationalist China and Chiang Kai-shek, and the myth of the democratic Chinese Communists.

Using almost the same language, McCarthy spoke to the Senate in March of the following year:

> Professor Jessup must therefore be credited by the American people with having pioneered the smear campaign against Nationalist China and Chiang Kai-shek, and with being the originator of the myth of the democratic Chinese Communists.

Also backing McCarthy were the Chicago *Tribune*, the Washington *Times-Herald*, the Hearst newspapers and their star columnists, Westbrook Pegler, George Sokolsky and Fulton Lewis, Jr., plus a group of oil-rich and ultraconservative Texans, who were most eager to assist the man from Wisconsin in his career, and William J. Goodwin, long a member of the anti-Semitic Christian Front.

And the China Lobby, so-called, could be numbered among McCarthy supporters. This private group was composed of enthusiastic backers of Chiang Kai-shek, professional lobbyists, friends, businessmen, all of whom stood to profit handsomely should the generalissimo be able to regain control of mainland China. The inefficiency and squalid corruption of Chiang's rule, as much responsible for the loss of the country as were the Communists, were ignored by the China Lobby in favor of a conspiratorial theory of Oriental history that simply failed to prove out.

Five members of Nationalist China's embassy in Washington controlled the China Lobby. Under the code name "Kung," they were responsible directly to Chiang. Some of their secret cables came into the possession of Senator Wayne Morse of Oregon, who had them translated.

One, dated December 5, 1949, despaired of relations between the United States and the Soviet Union disintegrating to the point of open conflict. It contained this remarkable sentence: "Our hope of a world war so as to rehabilitate our country is unpalatable to the [American] people."

Apparently the China Lobby had aimed to maneuver the United States into a war designed to return Chiang to power. Another cable sent three weeks after the start of fighting in Korea, repeated the same theme: "Whether the Chinese Communists send troops to Korea or not is of secondary importance, but the war in South Korea will be extended in any case."

Another cable, dated August 24, 1949, stated: "In the past years we have been very patient with General [George C.] Marshall, but he has never changed his attitude toward us. . . . But in order to avoid a direct break with the American administration, it is better for us not to attack him personally."

The China Lobby, however, had no objection if a Senator of the United States made such an attack, and Joe McCarthy would oblige them in less than two years.

The parade of witnesses before the Tydings committee went on until April 6, 1950, offering very little in the way of support for McCarthy's charges. Finally Owen Lattimore testified in his own behalf. He denied ever having been a Communist or of having followed Communst doctrine. Impressed by his testimony, Senator Tydings decided to end the affair.

"Dr. Lattimore," he said. "Your case has been designated the number-one case in the charges made by Senator McCarthy. You have been called, substantially if not accurately, the top Red spy agent in America. We have been told that, if we had access to certain files . . . this would be shown.

"As chairman of this committee, I owe it to you and to the country to tell you that four of the five members of this committee, in the presence of Mr. J. Edgar Hoover, had a complete summary of your file made available to them. . . . At the conclusion of the reading of that summary, it was the universal opinion of all of the members of the committee present and all others in the room that there was nothing in that file to show that you were a Communist or had ever been a Communist, or that you were in any way connected with any espionage. . . . The FBI file puts you completely, up to this moment at least, in the clear."

Asked for his response, McCarthy fired back. "Either Tydings hasn't seen the file, or he is lying. There is no other alternative."

Stand or fall on the Lattimore case, he had vowed, but McCarthy did neither. Instead, he struck out with vigor and bombast, issuing almost daily pronouncements and press releases, making speeches. There seemed to be no one in the Senate who dared oppose him, fearful that he might turn on them. Even when McCarthy's attacks were directed at the Secretary of State, Democrats seldom dared risk his ire by defending the Secretary. As for the Republicans, they, for the most part, regarded McCarthy as a crude, somewhat vulgar, but effective political weapon. They were, of course, most anxious to undercut the Democrat Party's hold on the electorate and felt McCarthy was successfully doing this.

But not all Senators were afraid. One who was not was both a Republican and a woman, Margaret Chase Smith. Slight, silver-haired, she spoke in the distinctive accents of her native Maine when she delivered a lecture to her fellow Senators that came to be known as the Republican Declaration of Conscience. It was cosigned by a small group of liberals: Wayne Morse of Oregon, Irving Ives of New York, George Aiken of Vermont, Charles Tobey of New Hampshire, Edward Thye of Minnesota and Robert Hendrickson of New Jersey.

Senator Smith said in part:

> I think it is high time that we remembered that we have sworn to uphold and defend the Constitution. I think it is high time that we remembered that the Constitution, as amended, speaks not only of the freedom of speech but also of trial by jury instead of trial by accusation. . . .
>
> Those of us who shout the loudest about Americanism in making character assassinations are all too frequently those who, by our own words and acts, ignore some of the basic principles of Americanism—
>
> The right to criticize.
> The right to hold unpopular beliefs.
> The right to protest.
> The right of independent thought.
>
> The exercise of these rights should not cost one single American citizen his reputation or his right to a livelihood nor should he be in danger of losing his reputation or livelihood merely because he happens to know someone who holds unpopular beliefs. Who of us does not? Otherwise none of us could call our souls our own. Otherwise thought control would have set in.

The Declaration of Conscience voiced the fear of the seven Senators of the confusion in the country, and they criticized the Administration for contributing to the situation. Republicans all, they went on to accuse their own party of "selfish political exploitation of fear, bigotry, ignorance and intolerance."

> To this extent, Democrats and Republicans alike have unwittingly, but undeniably, played directly into the Communist design of "confuse, divide, and conquer."
> It is high time that we stopped thinking politically as Republicans and Democrats about elections and started thinking patriotically as Americans about national security based on individual freedom. It is high time that we all stopped being tools and victims of totalitarian techniques—techniques that, if continued here unchecked, will surely end what we have come to cherish as the American way of life.

When Senator Smith finished speaking, a mere handful of Republicans and even fewer Democrats came over to congratulate her. The others feared the wrath of the junior Senator from Wisconsin and with an election on the horizon were taking no chances.

As for Joe McCarthy, the Declaration angered him, but not for long. Each new accusation created new headlines, made his name better known in every district and precinct across the country. He began to visit different cities, speaking to larger and larger groups about the Communist menace, his lecture fees climbing swiftly into the four-figure bracket. Patriotism for him had become profitable.

VII

A BANDIT RAID

IN THE UNITED STATES IT WAS SATURDAY, JUNE 24, 1950, A warm, slow day presaging the hot summer to come. Government workers fled the oppressive heat of Washington early, hoping for some respite from the cares of office over the weekend. But at the State Department there was increasing activity, the phones ringing all afternoon with calls from insistent newspapermen.

"There are reports of trouble in Korea. What's the real story?"

State had no such information came the persistent answer.

"Does General MacArthur in Tokyo report anything?"

There had been no word from the commander of Far Eastern forces or from the embassy in Seoul, capital of South Korea, or from anyone else, the inquirers were told. The reports were apparently rumors. If anything were to break, the press would be informed at once. It went on that way throughout the drowsy afternoon.

Bradley Connors, officer in charge of public affairs for the

State Department's Far Eastern Bureau, spent the day with his family in their Washington apartment. It was just past 8 P.M. when the phone rang. Connors answered. It was the United Press. Reports from the scene, the UP man insisted, indicated that there had been a major North Korean attack on the Republic of Korea. Connors hung up and tried to place a direct call to Seoul; the circuits were closed. He hurried to his office. An hour later, from the embassy in Seoul, came an official cable:

NORTH KOREAN FORCES INVADED REPUBLIC OF KOREA TERRITORY AT SEVERAL PLACES THIS MORNING. . . . IT WOULD APPEAR FROM THE NATURE OF THE ATTACK AND THE MANNER IN WHICH IT WAS LAUNCHED THAT IT CONSTITUTES AN ALL-OUT OFFENSIVE AGAINST THE REPUBLIC OF KOREA.

Connors began alerting official America.

Korea had long been recognized as a sensitive area, its strategic location on the Asian mainland making it a source of contention between rival political factions. Japan and China had warred over control of the peninsula in 1890–95, and Japan and Russia had clashed in 1904–05 because of the Czar's interference in the region. Finally, in 1910 Korea was occupied by Japan and remained so until liberated in 1945 by the Allied victory in the Pacific.

In 1943 at Cairo, Roosevelt, Churchill and Chiang Kai-shek issued a statement calling for a "free and independent" Korea. Joseph Stalin endorsed the call at Potsdam. At the close of the war against Japan, Russian troops went into Korea and accepted the surrender of all Japanese soldiers above the thirty-eighth parallel; United States forces did likewise south of the parallel.

From the American point of view, this division was only temporary, and over the next two years efforts were made to consolidate the country into a single democracy. The Russians, however, seemed to have no interest in uniting Korea, except on their own terms.

Frustrated by the recalcitrance of the Soviets, the United States turned over the problem to the United Nations, and the General Assembly called for national elections in Korea. But the U. N. Temporary Commission on Korea was kept out of the North, and so in August, 1948, elections were conducted only in the South. The Republic of Korea was established with Syngman Rhee, a despotic old nationalist, as president.

In 1949, the Soviet occupiers announced creation of the Democratic People's Republic of Korea in the North and soon afterward withdrew their troops. That same year, the United States removed the last of its combat forces from South Korea, though some soldiers remained with Syngman Rhee in an advisory capacity.

Soon after, North Korea commenced a dangerous game, raiding across the border, sometimes in force with as many as fifteen hundred men. By spring, 1950, intelligence reports claimed that with Soviet help the North Koreans were strong enough to launch a full-scale invasion whenever they chose.

Though Korea had been one of many likely trouble spots in the world back in 1947, the United States Joint Chiefs of Staff had marked it as being of minor concern and Congress, accepting this appraisal, had gone on to reject President Truman's request for $60 million in economic aid for that country.

Early in 1950, Secretary of State Dean Acheson spoke to members of the National Press Club about Far Eastern strategy. He described a "defensive perimeter" in the Pacific Ocean running from the Philippine Islands to Okinawa to Japan and on to the Aleutian Islands, off the coast of Alaska. Any attack on these places, or points east of them, he said, would bring an immediate military response from the United States.

As for Korea and other potential trouble spots outside the perimeter, Acheson said, ". . . it must be clear that no person can guarantee these areas against military attack. But it must also be clear that such a guarantee is hardly sensible or necessary within the realm of practical relationship. Should an attack occur—one hesitates to say where such an armed attack could come from—the initial reliance must be on the people attacked to resist it and then upon the commitments of the entire civilized world under the charter of the United Nations, which so far has not proved a weak reed to lean on by any people who are determined to protect their independence against outside aggression."

The Secretary's words were ambiguous—he had promised neither to assist nor to refrain from assisting any nation attacked. His words would eventually return to haunt him—and the nation.

As soon as Dean Acheson learned of the outbreak of fighting in Korea, he began taking steps to insure the sovereignty of Syngman Rhee's government. A call was made to U. N. Secretary General Trygve Lie requesting an emergency session of the General Assembly. Cables were dispatched to United States embassies, alerting them and ordering ambassadors to seek the support of their host countries in putting up a united front against the aggression. And, of course, the President was informed.

Years later, Mr. Truman was to say of this tense period: "Communism was acting in Korea just as Hitler, Mussolini and the Japanese had acted ten, fifteen and twenty years earlier. If this was allowed to go unchallenged, it would mean a third world war. It was also clear to me that the foundations and principles of the United Nations were at stake unless this unprovoked attack on Korea could be stopped."

That Sunday afternoon, the U. N. Security Council met in emergency session and by a vote of 9 to 0 branded the North Korean invasion "a breach of the peace." Russia was absent from the session, having boycotted the Security Council since January because of the U. N.'s refusal to seat Communist China.

At the White House, the President met with his advisers. He listened to their reports, entertained their recommendations, began issuing orders.

General MacArthur, stationed in Tokyo, was told to evacuate all American civilians from Korea and to supply fighter air cover to protect this operation. The planes were to remain below the thirty-eighth parallel, if possible. In addition, MacArthur was to deliver to the army of South Korea ammunition and supplies.

The U. S. Seventh Fleet was ordered to sail for the Formosa Strait and directed to stem the spread of the conflict in that area.

By Monday it was clear that the North Koreans were ignoring the cease-fire order. They moved down the peninsula in a six-pronged advance that heralded the fall of the Republic of Korea. South Korean soldiers were unable to slow the invaders. Observers everywhere agreed that the outcome in Korea depended on what the United States would do.

After conferring for long hours with his "war cabinet," President Truman announced his decision:

> In Korea the Government forces, which were armed to prevent border raids and to preserve internal security, were attacked by invading forces from North Korea. The Security Council . . . called upon the invading troops to cease hostilities and to withdraw to the thirty-eighth parallel. This they have not done, but on the contrary have pressed the attack. The Security Council called upon all members of the United Nations to render every assistance to the United Nations in the execution of this resolution. In this circumstance, I

have ordered United States air and sea forces to give the Korean Government cover and support.

The attack upon Korea makes it plain beyond all doubt that Communism has passed beyond the use of subversion to conquer independent nations and will now use armed invasion and war. It has defied the orders of the Security Council . . . issued to preserve international peace and security. In these circumstances the occupation of Formosa by Communist forces would be a direct threat to the security of the Pacific area and to United States forces performing their lawful and necessary functions in that area.

Accordingly I have ordered the Seventh Fleet to prevent any attack on Formosa. As a corollary of this action I am calling upon the Chinese Government of Formosa to cease all air and sea operations against the mainland. The Seventh Fleet will see that this is done. The determination of the future status of Formosa must await the restoration of security in the Pacific, a peace settlement with Japan, or consideration by the United Nations.

I have also directed that United States forces in the Philippines be strengthened and that military assistance to the Philippine Government be accelerated.

I have similarly directed acceleration in the furnishing of military assistance to the forces of France and the associated states in Indochina and the dispatch of a military mission to provide close working relations with those forces.

I know that all members of the United Nations will consider carefully the consequences of this latest aggression in Korea in defiance of the Charter of the United Nations. A return to the rule of force in international affairs would have far-reaching effects. The United States will continue to uphold the rule of law.

I have instructed Ambassador Austin, as the representative of the United States to the Security Council, to report these steps to the Council.

On June 27, the Security Council adopted a resolution which recommended that "the members of the United Nations furnish such assistance to the Republic of Korea as may be necessary to repel the armed attack and to restore international peace and security in the area."

Yugoslavia voted against the resolution; the Soviet Union, whose veto could have killed it, remained absent.

In Korea, disaster was settling over the southern portion of that unhappy land. The R. O. K. troops, badly mauled, fell steadily back. The invaders took over the city of Seoul, and it seemed the country must inevitably be overrun.

John Foster Dulles, who was then a consultant to the Secretary of State, had just returned from the Orient and talks with General MacArthur. He was convinced that South Korea was unable, on its own, to repel the enemy. In this, Defense Secretary Louis A. Johnson concurred. On their information and recommendations, the President acted. He commanded General MacArthur to allow his planes to fly north of the thirty-eighth parallel, their strikes to be limited to military targets. Also, MacArthur was to put American ground troops into Korea to secure airfields and port facilities and to create a system of communications with the air forces.

On Wednesday, Senator Robert A. Taft rose in the Senate to address himself to United States' participation in Korea. He gave reluctant support to the enterprise, seeking to make political capital.

"I approve of the changes now made in our foreign policy, I

approve of the general policies outlined in the President's statement. . . . I suggest, however, that any Secretary of State who has been so reversed . . . had better resign. . . ."

This obvious reference to Dean Acheson and his limited Pacific "defense perimeter" drew considerable approval from critics of the Administration. Prominent among those applauding was Senator Joe McCarthy.

On the following day, the President conducted a press conference at the White House. The following exchange took place:

"Mr. President, everybody is asking in this country, are we or are we not at war?" a reporter asked.

"We are not at war."

"Mr. President, could you elaborate on that statement 'We are not at war,' and could we use it in quotes?"

"Yes, I will allow you to use that in quotes. The Republic of Korea was set up with United Nations help. It was unlawfully attacked by a bunch of bandits which are neighbors, in North Korea. The United Nations held a meeting and asked the members to go to the relief of the Korean Republic, and the members of the United Nations are going to the relief of the Korean Republic to suppress a bandit raid on the Republic of Korea. That is all there is to it."

"Would it be correct to call it a police action under the United Nations?"

"Yes," Mr. Truman replied. "That is exactly what it amounts to."

Sixteen countries were to join in this police action, the United States assuming about 90 percent of the responsibility. More than 150,000 American casualties would be taken during the fighting, and the phrase "police action" would return subsequently to cause the President and his party considerable political trouble.

On Friday of that same week, the situation in the war zone appeared to be disintegrating. General MacArthur, just back from a reconnaissance of combat conditions, sent a blunt appraisal to Washington:

> THE SOUTH KOREAN FORCES ARE IN CONFUSION. . . . THEY WERE UNPREPARED FOR ATTACK BY ARMOR AND AIR. . . . IT IS ESSENTIAL THAT THE ENEMY ADVANCE BE HELD OR ITS IMPETUS WILL THREATEN THE OVERRUNNING OF ALL KOREA. . . . THE ONLY ASSURANCE FOR HOLDING THE PRESENT LINE AND THE ABILITY TO REGAIN LATER THE LOST GROUND IS THROUGH THE INTRODUCTION OF UNITED STATES GROUND COMBAT FORCES INTO THE KOREAN BATTLE AREA. . . . IF AUTHORIZED IT IS MY INTENTION TO . . . PROVIDE FOR A POSSIBLE BUILD-UP TO A TWO DIVISION STRENGTH FROM THE TROOPS IN JAPAN FOR AN EARLY COUNTEROFFENSIVE.

The President provided the asked-for authorization. At twenty-two minutes past one that afternoon, not quite six full days after the first shots had been fired, orders were issued that irrevocably committed the United States. A naval blockade of the North was to be established; planes, armor and infantry were sent to the battle front.

Two facts were evident: the United States was forcibly demonstrating that it meant to confront and turn back aggression; and for the first time, a President had led the country into a shooting war on his own authority. Repercussions were already being heard, and nothing could ever be the same.

VIII

PAYMENT, POSTCARDS AND A PICTURE

THE NEWS WAS GRIM. THE NORTH KOREANS, OUTNUMBERING the UN forces, were steadily advancing. The UN soldiers fought valiantly but were unable to stem the tide. Here economy-minded Congressmen, who had consistently hacked away at proposed budgets, could view the results of their handiwork—poorly trained and equipped American soldiers were being sent into combat and were unable to do the job.

Eventually, with the arrival of additional men and machines, the balance of battle shifted. On September 15, in a brilliant land-sea operation, troops were put ashore at Inchon, near the western end of the thirty-eighth parallel. They moved inland, and suddenly large numbers of North Korean soldiers began to surrender. Those that did not fled north, and the UN forces went after them, crossing the parallel, advancing deeper into North Korea. On November 24, General MacArthur ordered a "final" attack, with which he intended to crush all resistance

FREEDOM IN JEOPARDY

and reunify North and South Korea under the United Nations. "The war," MacArthur told reporters, "very definitely is coming to an end shortly."

Earlier, Chou En-lai, Communist China's Foreign Minister, had warned the world that, if the U. N. carried the war into North Korea, China would enter the fray.

MacArthur's intelligence chief, General Charles A. Willoughby, termed this "probably in a category of diplomatic blackmail." His commanding officer concurred.

Since the start of hostilities, it had become increasingly clear that General MacArthur and his civilian chief, the President of the United States, viewed the situation in Korea from entirely different perspectives, were aiming at different goals. Washington was concerned about the possible entrance into the conflict of China, with its unlimited manpower, and there was equal concern about possible Russian intervention. Vladivostok was only forty miles beyond the eastern tip of Korea. Let Moscow feel threatened, and Soviet troops might join the fighting. A confrontation between the great powers might easily trigger World War III.

The American Joint Chiefs of Staff cautioned MacArthur: Do nothing to provoke the Russians or the Chinese massed across the Yalu River. Further, they suggested that operations north of the thirty-eighth parallel be left to South Korea's soldiers.

Civilian leaders viewed Korea as an effort to *contain* an aggressor, not to destroy him. They saw it as a fight with limited objectives, hoping to prevent a larger and uncontrollable conflict.

Then Assistant Secretary of State Dean Rusk put it this way: "What we are trying to do is to maintain peace and security without a general war. We are saying to the aggressors, 'You will not be allowed to get away with your crime. You must stop it.' At the same time we are trying to prevent a general conflagration which would consume the very things we are now trying to defend."

In a later comment, General MacArthur displayed an inability to understand this approach. "That policy," he said, "seems to me to introduce a new concept into military operations—the concept of appeasement, the concept that, when you use force, you can limit the force."

For very long MacArthur had been virtually autonomous in his commands. A man of great military skills with a vanity equally large, the general frequently displayed scorn for political Washington. He had not been in the United States since 1937, had claimed the Far East as a sort of private province, looked unkindly on anyone who dared to question his decisions. He strongly objected to the concept of limited war and believed Chiang Kai-shek from Formosa should strike at mainland China.

That summer MacArthur dispatched a message to the Veterans of Foreign Wars describing his own concept of how to deal with problems in the Orient and the Pacific. A direct contradiction to official policy, this was in itself an insubordinate act. Though it had already been made public, President Truman ordered MacArthur to withdraw the message, and he did so.

Even as the tempo of fighting in Korea was stepped up, something very profound and radical began to occur within the ranks of the United States Army. To date, army units had been formed, among other considerations, along racial lines, a reflection of American society itself. Negroes were assigned to all-black units, Caucasians to all-white units.

Sergeant John Rice was killed in Korea. His body was shipped home only to be refused burial in the Sioux City Memorial Park because Sergeant Rice was not white. He was a Winnebago Indian. President Truman learned of the incident and invited Sergeant Rice's wife to bury him in Arlington National Cemetery. Of this slight to a man whose ancestors had lived in America before any white man reached these shores, the Cleveland *Plain-Dealer* wrote: "It is high time we stopped this business. We can't do it as decent human beings, and we can't do it as a nation trying to sell democracy to a world full of nonwhite peoples."

The Army, which had been slow in fulfilling a directive to eliminate segregation in its ranks, began to change. As fighting in Korea intensified, keeping blacks and whites separate was a time-consuming practice, too much trouble, too inefficient. In the interest of competence, segregation had to go, and go it did, despite the trepidation of traditionalists in and out of the service.

The results surprised them. In the past, all-black units had seldom proved to be dependable in combat. Now, however, in integrated units, black men fought as well as—and in many cases better than—white soldiers. Treated as equals when it came to reward or to responsibility, black men acted accordingly.

Even as the Army changed, so did civilian institutions in the vicinity of military establishments. Restaurants, taxi companies, night clubs, churches, motels—all began to soften their restrictive policies, to adapt to the changing realities.

Meanwhile, in Korea, the situation grew increasingly delicate. Reports filtered in of troop movements, of military units in great numbers assembling along the Manchurian border. Concerned about this as well as other matters, President Truman decided that it was time he and his field commander met face-to-face. Both men flew to Wake Island for the confrontation which took place on October 15. A secretary made an unauthorized transcript of the exchange between the two men.

"What are the chances for Chinese or Soviet interference?" the President wanted to know.

"Very little. Had they interfered in the first or second months, it would have been decisive. We are no longer fearful of their intervention. . . . If the Chinese tried to get down to Pyongyang, there would be the greatest slaughter."

When asked what additional support Washington could provide, MacArthur replied, "No commander in the history of war has ever had more complete and adequate support from all agencies in Washington than I have."

But soon MacArthur would say otherwise.

Korea seemed to affect Senator Joe McCarthy very little. He was having difficulties of his own. In July, the Tydings committee made public its report, the majority referring to McCarthy's charges of Communists in Government in dramatic terms:

> At a time when American blood is again being shed to preserve our dream of freedom, we are constrained fearlessly and frankly to call the charges, and the methods employed to give them ostensible validity, what they truly are: a fraud and a hoax perpetrated on the Senate of the United States and the American people. . . . In such a disillusioning setting, we appreciate as never before our Bill of Rights, a free press, and the heritage of freedom that has made this nation great.

Furious at this public rebuke by his peers, McCarthy decided to punish Millard Tydings for chairing the committee. Tydings was up for reelection in Maryland that autumn, and Joe McCarthy intended to play a major role in that campaign.

Running against Democrat Senator Tydings would be John Marshall Butler, a Baltimore lawyer with no previous political experience, an unlikely winner. McCarthy arranged a meeting with Butler. Also present were Cornelius Mundy, Butler's treasurer, Jean Kerr, McCarthy's secretary whom he later married, and Robert Morris, a lawyer who had been the Republican counsel on the Tydings committee. Plans were made to defeat Millard Tydings.

With McCarthy and Ruth McCormick Miller, publisher of the Washington *Times-Herald*, plotting most of the moves, the attack on the incumbent Senator got under way. Tydings never had a chance. Half a million copies of a specially written and printed tabloid newspaper attacking him were distributed, perhaps the single most effective weapon used against him.

Frank M. Smith, assistant to Mrs. Miller, who became Butler's assistant after the election, later testified that most of the written material was supplied by Senator McCarthy's office. Photographs came from the *Times-Herald*. One picture, showing Senator Tydings and former Communist Party boss Earl Browder in a friendly talk, may have been the key element in the smear campaign. The caption read:

> Communist leader Earl Browder, shown at left in this composite picture, was a star witness at the Tydings committee hearings, and was cajoled into saying Owen Lattimore and others accused of disloyalty were not Communists. Tydings (right) answered, "Oh, thank you, sir." Browder testified in the best interests of those accused, naturally.

Many readers of the campaign handout may not have fully understood that the composite picture was in fact a doctored photograph, an amalgam of other pictures, created in order to give the impression that Browder and Tydings had actually been in conversation, as the deliberately misleading caption indicated. This imaginative work was executed in the *Times-Herald* art department. Even campaign treasurer Mundy admitted that he found the photograph to be "stupid, puerile and in bad taste."

A front-page story in the tabloid went further to misrepresent Millard Tydings' position as chairman of the Senate Armed Services Committee, charging that he had failed to prevent the war in Korea. [The responsibility, of course, had not been Senator Tydings' any more than it had been Senator McCarthy's.]

FREEDOM IN JEOPARDY

The tabloid story went on to accuse Tydings and the Armed Services Committee of spending only two hundred dollars (for baling wire) for armaments in Korea. In truth, prior to the outbreak of fighting, $495,700,000 in supplies and arms had been dispatched to Syngman Rhee.

Another vital factor in defeating Tydings was a postcard campaign—half a million cards, all supposedly handwritten by Candidate Butler himself. But John Marshall Butler had no time for such details. Instead the cards were inscribed by crews of women under the authority of a Baltimore printer, William Fedder. When it looked as if Fedder, and his teams of writers, might miss the mailing deadline, Butler tried to rekindle the printer's enthusiasm by sending him this note:

> At this time I want to give you my personal assurance that I do guarantee payment for any of your services that have not been paid for at the time the campaign is completed. This assurance applies to materials that have been delivered and to materials that were not shipped in time for use in the campaign.

In writing and signing this missive, Butler opened himself to serious trouble. Maryland's corrupt-practices law prohibited a candidate from spending in excess of $5,000 in his campaigns. The postcards alone cost over $11,000.

Word of Butler's self-incriminating note reached Senator McCarthy, who reassured the candidate. There was no need for Butler to concern himself about the note; McCarthy's people would retrieve the threatening piece of paper.

Printer Fedder later testified under oath before a Senate committee investigating the Butler campaign as to what followed. He told of intimidating words and threatening actions, of riding around aimlessly in a car with some of McCarthy's aides, becoming sick with fright.

Eventually Fedder signed two statements given to him by Don Surine, a McCarthy assistant. One concerned itself with the job Fedder was doing for them, and the other was an attempt to nullify candidate Butler's guarantee note, saying that Butler owed the printer no money.

The question of the economics of Butler's campaign came under scrutiny. When it was revealed that many expenditures had simply not been listed, as they should have been according to state law, Jon Jonkel, a high-powered Chicago press agent imported to serve Butler as campaign manager [also in violation of Maryland state law] hastened to declare $27,100 in out-of-state contributions—long after the legal deadline for filing lists of contributions had expired. Among the contributors were Alfred Kohlberg, $1,000, Senator Owen Brewster, $1,000, Ruth McCormick Miller, $5,000. For his role in all this, Jonkel was charged in a Baltimore court where he pleaded guilty on six counts and was fined $5,000.

In commenting on the printed tabloid, including the fraudulent photograph, investigators of the Maryland campaign reported it as being larded with "misleading half-truths, misrepresentations, and false innuendoes that maliciously and without foundation attacked the loyalty and patriotism not only of former Senator Millard Tydings, who won the Distinguished Service Cross for battlefield heroism in World War I, but also the entire membership of the Senate Armed Services Committee in 1950."

The campaign investigating committee went on to declare that there had been two different campaigns in Maryland: "One was the dignified 'front street' campaign conducted by candidate Butler. . . . The other was the despicable 'back street' type of campaign, which usually, if exposed in time, backfires."

But the "back street" campaign was not revealed in time, and thanks to the efforts of Joe McCarthy and his men, Millard Tydings lost the election.

Commonweal, a respected Catholic lay journal, wrote of the Maryland campaign, and of Senator McCarthy:

> The issue here is not whether or not Communism must be fought at home: it must. The issue is whether or not we must have the intelligence and the courage to do it in the American way, or whether we will leave the job—and our liberties—to a man who runs along the back streets to do his cheating when he hasn't the stuff it takes to do things the straight and open way.

Joe McCarthy paid little heed to such criticism. He counted Maryland as a stirring victory, and it did not matter to him whether the voters of the state had been dealt with fairly. The Maryland election, he boasted, was "one of the cleanest campaigns in the country." To him, morality was anything that succeeded.

To nervous politicians across the country the true message of Maryland was written in blazing letters for all to see: Oppose the junior Senator from Wisconsin, and the same thing could happen again—to you.

McCarthyism cast its gloomy shadow across the land.

IX

THE GENERAL AND THE PRESIDENT

ON NOVEMBER 24, 1950, GENERAL MACARTHUR ANNOUNCED the launching of his final offensive, one that would win the war. On the next day, as if in response, units of the Communist Chinese army virtually wiped out the Republic of Korea's Second Corps and sent the United States Twenty-fourth Division fleeing across the Chongchon River.

China, as so many people had feared for so long it would do, had joined the fight. An entirely new conflict had begun.

This forced United States leadership to reassess matters. Clearly, the attempt to inflict a political settlement on Korea by force of arms had failed and might now never be possible. Instead, the United States found itself in a war which it could not win, and from which it was unable to extricate itself. Here was a distressing dilemma for a nation accustomed to victory in its wars.

There was more to concern politicians and the people alike. In order to provide General MacArthur with the troops, planes and supplies he desired, America might find it necessary to pull back from its commitments in other strategic areas of the globe. There was every reason to believe that the Communists would like very much to engage the United States in a long, bloody, and in the end futile, conflict, the kind of fight that China with her population of more than five hundred million could afford, the kind of fight that would drain America's resources, human and material. To complicate matters, the continued support of the United Nations and its member countries was vital in order to continue the Korean struggle.

But Douglas MacArthur did not change. With a bloody impasse existing on the battlefield around the thirty-eighth parallel, he continued a sustained attack against his civilian superiors, demonstrating minimum comprehension of why he and his men had been sent to Korea. Up to now a reluctant subject for press interviews, the general began to make himself more available to reporters. His difficulties, he announced in December, 1950, were solely due to "the extraordinary inhibitions . . . without precedent in military history . . ." which prevented him from extending the war into the "privileged sanctuary" of the Chinese. At another time he was quoted as saying that his failure to win "results largely from the acceptance of military odds without precedent in history—the odds of permitting offensive action without defensive retaliation."

When this very obvious criticism of governmental policy reached President Truman, he became angry, saying later that he "should have fired MacArthur then and there." Instead, another directive was sent to the general insisting that "no speech, press release or public statement" was to be issued by him in the future regarding foreign policy unless cleared first with the State Department or, when concerned with military policy, with the Department of Defense.

At about the same time, the President asked the Congress for additional monies for defense, emphasizing the necessity for shoring up the North Atlantic Treaty Organization (NATO). He also declared a national emergency, which allowed a faster buildup of the military establishment. But this was not, he made clear, "total mobilization."

At the U. N., the General Assembly adopted a resolution aimed at obtaining a cease-fire in Korea. This the Chinese rejected.

To increase further President Truman's burden, Republicans in both houses of Congress asked him to dismiss Secretary of State Dean Acheson on the grounds that "he had lost the confidence of the country." Acheson stayed on. But here was a manifestation of the widening division in the nation, a reflection of the ongoing attacks of Senator McCarthy.

Encouraged by McCarthy's activities, by public unrest, by a climate of deepening fear and suspicion, the professional bigots and hatemongers became openly bolder. The ground had been prepared for them, and they proceeded to plant their hatred and distrust, to turn neighbors against each other, groups of Americans against other groups.

Senator McCarthy blamed Communists for the worsening world situation, for the ills of America. The bigots did more than that. They blamed the Jews and the blacks. They blamed the poor for being poor and the rich for being rich. They blamed a world that refused to remain static on the accents of the foreign-born, on the cast of their skin, the odd set of their eyes. They blamed everyone who did not agree with them, blamed every idea which was not in perfect accord with their own. And they spoke darkly of sinister plots and conspiracies.

Much of this coalesced and surfaced with the nomination of Mrs. Anna Rosenberg, a woman of fine reputation with a solid background in state and Federal government, to be Assistant Secretary of Defense. The Reverend Wesley Swift, a known anti-Semite, delivered "evidence" to Senator McCarthy that Mrs. Rosenberg was a Communist.

McCarthy dispatched his investigator, Don Surine, to gather more information. With him was Edward Nellor, an employee of similar responsibilities for conservative newscaster Fulton Lewis, Jr. They paid a midnight visit to Benjamin Freedman, an impassioned anti-Zionist, carrying a letter from Gerald L. K. Smith, a man whose anti-Semitic declarations were in the public record. The letter began: "Congratulations on the terrific job you are doing to keep the Zionist Jew Anna M. Rosenberg from becoming director of the Pentagon. . . ."

With Benjamin Freedman's help, McCarthy's legmen found an ex-Communist, Ralph DeSola, who identified Mrs. Rosenberg as a one-time Communist Party member. It looked as if the Senator had uncovered a real security lapse at the highest levels, and it was an opportunity he knew how to exploit. But Mrs. Rosenberg refused to become a docile victim. She fought back angrily.

Of DeSola, she said, "He is a liar. I would like to lay my hands on that man. . . . I have never been a member of the John Reed Club; I have never been a Communist; I have never sympathized with Communists; I have spent my life trying to do something to help my country."

Witnesses were called to a Senate Committee and the "case" against Anna Rosenberg began to crumble. James Magraw, a former Communist, denied DeSola had met Mrs. Rosenberg through him, as had been asserted. William Harris, characterized by DeSola as an ex-FBI agent, proved never to have been with the bureau. He swore that he knew nothing about any Communist connections of Mrs. Rosenberg. When other witnesses also denied the accusations, even Benjamin Freedman was forced to admit that he held no evidence against the lady. Fulton Lewis, Jr., began to back off, to offer explanations for what was happening, and Senator McCarthy quickly dropped the matter.

Then the FBI learned that someone named Anna Rosenberg, who was then living on the Pacific Coast, had attended a meeting of the John Reed Club (a Communist organization) some twenty years earlier. But there was no possible connection between her and the nominee. Eventually Mrs. Rosenberg was confirmed for the Assistant Defense Secretary's post, and Joe McCarthy voted enthusiastically for her.

Setbacks of this kind did not give McCarthy pause. He pushed on, managing one way or another to keep his name in the headlines, his image as a protector of the nation's security in everyone's mind. During a Senatorial discussion of his own defiance of the Subcommittee on Privileges and Elections, he went on the offensive by demanding that the investigation turn its attention to Senator William Benton of Connecticut, who had earlier asked for McCarthy's expulsion from the Senate.

On another occasion, McCarthy got into a fist fight with columnist Drew Pearson, a critic who had dared to question him about his difficulties with the Wisconsin state tax authorities.

McCarthy possessed the rare talent of obtaining publicity, no matter how far removed he might be from an event. When Nathan Pusey was named President of Harvard University, McCarthy injected this irrelevant thought into the public prints: "I do not think Dr. Pusey is or has been a member of the Communist Party."

And if things went too slowly for the Senator, he would hold a morning press conference at which he would announce that he intended to conduct an afternoon press conference.

Once, on the Senate floor, he claimed to be reading from a letter written by Owen Lattimore. He would be pleased, he said, to show the revealing document to any Senator who cared to study it. Senator Lehman rose to accept the offer. "I yield no further," McCarthy said hurriedly. Actually, he had no such letter; he had invented it to suit his purpose of the moment, as was later revealed.

Thus did McCarthy continue to bury the truth under an avalanche of accusations and allegations that misled and confused, spread uncertainty and fear. Newsman Elmer Davis said of this technique, "I can't afford to hire a full-time specialist to keep up with what McCarthy has said." Nor could anyone else, and so McCarthy advanced, holding high his so-called banner of patriotism, challenging the loyalty and good intentions of anyone who dared to question his methods.

McCarthy's singular approach to domestic security was mirrored by Douglas MacArthur's intransigence in Korea. The general continued to make known his personal ideas of how the war should be run. He said again that he wanted to destroy China's industry by unlimited air and sea bombardment, to use Chiang Kai-shek's army, to allow Chiang to make diversionary attacks on the Chinese mainland, to blockade China.

These suggestions were diametrically opposite to the declared limited-war policy of the United States and of the United Nations. MacArthur also ignored the mutual-defense pact that existed between China and the Soviet Union and the possibility that the Soviet Union might enter the conflict if the Chinese mainland were to be attacked.

Once again instructions went from the Joint Chiefs of Staff to MacArthur: Fight a limited war. And from President Truman came another explanation of the complex world politics that helped shape American policy in Korea and elsewhere. Once more the Commander-in-Chief detailed the goals of the United States: to display firmness in the face of Communist aggression; to prove the strength and flexibility of the U. N., and by doing so, affirm the convictions of the struggling countries of Europe and the Middle East that the United Nations and the United States would similarly help them.

Nevertheless, the President came under fire at home. Former President Herbert Hoover insisted that we should turn away from foreign involvements and convert America into a fortress, and Senator Taft continued to argue for the Congressional prerogative to declare war. Korea was labeled Truman's War.

There were other pressing domestic difficulties, too. Inflation was once again eroding the value of the dollar, and when the President acted to curb it by reinstituting limited price and wage controls, there was a howl of displeasure from both industry and labor. Another railroad strike was threatened but, fortunately, it did not occur. Corruption was reported in the Reconstruction Finance Corporation. In Washington, there were revelations of gifts given in return for political favors, of deep freezes and mink coats.

Nor was the unsavory limited to Washington and politics. Three members of the championship basketball team of the City College of New York were exposed as having accepted bribes to rig the scores of some games. Before the sports scandal was over, it had spread to New York University, Long Island University, Kentucky, Bradley and Toledo Universities.

Then, scandal was exposed in West Point Academy, molder of officers and gentlemen for the Army. West Point—a place where character was all important, where men were trained to lead other men into combat, to defend the Republic. Ninety cadets were dismissed for cheating on examinations. They included an All America quarterback and eight other football players, plus members of other varsity teams. The son of the football coach, Earl Blaik, was among those named. In defending the dismissed cadets as "men of character," Coach Blaik remarked, "God help this country if we didn't play football. . . ."

Across the country, other young people got into trouble. The recorded rate of juvenile delinquency rose alarmingly. According to statistics, robbery, assault, housebreaking, drug use, sexual assaults, murder were done with increasing frequency by the young.

But the young were hardly the only ones breaking the law. A Senate committee under Senator Estes Kefauver of Kentucky was busy looking into the influence and extent of organized crime, and discovered that its tentacles reached into the highest of places as well as the lowest.

All sense of unity and purpose seemed to have evaporated. Americans desperately craved some solutions for the troubles at home and abroad, needed someone to blame. Fear being unreasoning, they were ready to blame almost anyone.

There was general agreement in Washington that no clear-cut victory was possible in Korea. The conclusion was equally obvious that some kind of a compromise had to be worked out, the appalling loss of life ended. Members of the Administration recognized the political danger inherent in possible peace negotiations, were certain the Republicans would cry "appeasement," would attack any diplomatic steps that might be taken toward peace. Nevertheless it had to be done. George Marshall, now Secretary of Defense, Secretary of State Dean Acheson, along with Dean Rusk, Assistant Secretary of State in charge of Far Eastern Affairs, and the Joint Chiefs prepared a statement to be issued by the President. This declared that, now that the aggressors were out of the Republic of Korea, back behind the thirty-eighth parallel, the U. N. would be amenable to a cease-fire and peace negotiations. Copies of the statement were distributed for consideration among each of the fourteen nations involved in Korea, and the text was radioed to General MacArthur. A covering message to the general said, "State planning Presidential announcement shortly that, with clearing of bulk of South Korea of aggression, U. N. now prepared to discuss conditions of settlement in Korea. Strong U. N. feeling persists that further diplomatic effort toward settlement should be made before any advance with major forces north of the thirty-eighth parallel. . . ."

The message left no room for doubt—the President was getting ready to negotiate a settlement at the highest diplomatic level, and the general was to support this effort by maintaining the military status quo.

Four days later, MacArthur acted on his own. He claimed to have frustrated the aggressive designs of the Chinese, despite being kept under "inhibitions and restrictions," insisted that, were he allowed to pursue his own military designs, China would be "doomed to imminent military collapse." Having threatened China with absolute destruction, he suggested how they might avoid that end:

> Within the area of my authority as the military commander, however, it would be needless to say that I stand ready at any time to confer in the field with the commander in chief of the enemy forces . . . to find means whereby realization of the military objectives of the United Nations in Korea might be accomplished without further bloodshed.

First, MacArthur had threatened to bring the war to China proper, in contradiction of his orders. Next he violated the directive that only routine statements were to be made by his headquarters without prior consent of his superiors. This done, he arbitrarily inserted himself into the most sensitive diplomatic maneuvers, then in progress. In each instance, he was challenging and superseding the authority of the President, who was Commander-in-Chief of the armed forces.

As if to underscore MacArthur's defiance of civilian authority, Joseph W. Martin, Minority Leader of the House of Representatives, read into the record a letter from the general. MacArthur had written of meeting force with maximum counterforce, that "here we fight Europe's war with arms while the diplomats there still fight it with words." He ended, "As you point out, we must win. There is no substitute for victory."

The criticism of Administration policy was obvious, the defiance of the President clear for all to see. Harry Truman, though willing to entertain a difference of opinion, an exchange of philosophies, was no man to tolerate insubordination.

At 1 A.M., Wednesday, April 11, 1951, General Douglas MacArthur, commanding general of the United States Army Forces, supreme commander for the Allied Powers in Japan, and commander-in-chief, United Nations Command, hero of the Philippines and of Bataan, leader of the war in the Pacific against the Japanese, was relieved of his command by Harry S. Truman, former captain of artillery, the President of the United States.

A reporter asked Senator Joe McCarthy for his reaction to Mr. Truman's action. The Senator said of the President, "The son of a bitch ought to be impeached."

X

A SUBSTITUTE FOR VICTORY

INEVITABLY THE SENATE INVESTIGATED GENERAL MACARTHUR'S dismissal. The general gave testimony for twenty-one hours and ten minutes. Also questioned were the Secretary of Defense, the Secretary of State, members of the Joint Chiefs. The eyes of the nation focused on the marble-walled Caucus Room of the Senate.

The image of Douglas MacArthur as a commander of lofty and correct military concepts made it almost impossible for most Senators to oppose him and his attitudes. There was a mythical aura to General MacArthur that had captured the popular imagination, and there were people who clamored for him to become the country's next President, the Man on a White Horse who would lead America back onto the road to truth and freedom.

For most Senators, the situation was made to order. It provided them with a chance to make political capital, to strike at things they didn't like, at the Administration, at Harry Truman.

As for MacArthur, at home or in Korea, he chose to perform in the same manner—attack, attack, attack.

He hit at the civilians in the Defense and State Departments who created foreign policy. He struck out at the Joint Chiefs, claiming that no difference existed between their ideas and his own, which was a provable distortion of fact.

"There is no policy," he lamented. "There is nothing, I tell you, no plan, no anything."

It was an easy claim to make but, as MacArthur continued to testify, it became apparent that the general had not always been correct in either theory or in practice. Also apparent were the vanity and arrogance that recognized no fallibility in himself while criticizing the human shortcomings of others.

In the end, there was the constitutional aspect of the dispute, something MacArthur and his supporters managed to ignore. The Founding Fathers had lodged ultimate power in all matters in elected civilian authority, in the President, that office being the symbol and the protector of the Constitution.

Eventually the furor subsided. The investigation ended. The general's dismissal was affirmed. Nevertheless, General MacArthur had served the nation long and well, and his final leave-taking before the Congress was charged with emotion and drama.

The afternoon of June 14, 1951, was waning when Senator Joe McCarthy spoke on the Senate floor, the ever-present bulging briefcase at his side. There were items in that case, he maintained, that would be valuable to the Senate Armed Services and the Foreign Relations Committees; both were then investigating American policy in the Orient. Some Senators might have believed McCarthy was about to unloose another defense of Douglas MacArthur. But the Senator was not concerned with either MacArthur or Far Eastern policy.

He was out to get a man, his aim to put an end to a long

and honorable career before its time had come. It was General of the Army George Catlett Marshall, formerly Secretary of State, presently Secretary of Defense, author of the Marshall Plan, whom he was after. He accused Marshall of being part of a "conspiracy so immense and an infamy so black as to dwarf any previous such venture in the history of man."

In a way this was the most daring and violent charge McCarthy ever made.

President Truman had described George Marshall as the "greatest living American." A man of unrivaled dignity and reputation, his patriotism and honesty never questioned, in his own style General Marshall was as much a symbol of greatness as General MacArthur had been in his. To attack Marshall seemed not only foolhardy but dangerous, for on the record he appeared unassailable.

Few Senators were on the floor of the Senate that day when McCarthy stood up to speak, and he never troubled to read all of his speech, but inserted it into the *Congressional Record* after uttering just a few sentences. He began by apologizing: "I have informed many Senators that in view of the fact that this speech is approximately 60,000 words, I do not expect them to sit and listen to it as I deliver it." He then proceeded to attack George Marshall as a traitor, characterizing him as a "man so steeped in falsehood who has recourse to the lie whenever it suits his convenience. . . ."

General Marshall's name soon became anathema to people who never troubled to read McCarthy's speech or to compare it with Marshall's actual record. Of that record, William Buckley, Jr., always a supporter of McCarthy, wrote with reluctant charity, "Almost all Marshall's decisions were backed by other military men and diplomats whose attitude . . . cannot be described as treasonable." Other Americans of high and low estate defended the general, without appreciable effect. The damage was done.

The McCarthy speech terminated Marshall's future usefulness to the country, soiled his reputation with falsehood and slander. To be named by Joe McCarthy was to a great many people proof of guilt. In their unreasoning fear and biased outlook, they suspended critical judgment and disregarded the legal safeguards and constitutional guarantees which form the framework of American liberty. Foremost among those, of course, are the right to face one's accuser and the assumption of an accused's innocence until his guilt is proved.

Much of this grew out of the peculiar charisma of Joe McCarthy and the hold he had gained over a large segment of the population, for in almost every instance his charges went unproved. The guilt or innocence of his victims became academic—except to them, their families and their friends.

McCarthy's support came from a broader base than just the wild fringes of society. To his Republican colleagues, he was a valuable tool making political profit of benefit to them all. Said Senator Taft, "The pro-Communist policies of the State Department fully justified Joe McCarthy in his demand for an investigation." But Taft knew that the State Department was *not* pro-Communist and further that McCarthy had never attacked the *policies* of the Department. Always it was *men* McCarthy attacked, individuals, many of whom never had any connection with the formulation of policy.

Throughout 1951, the recklessness continued and spread. With a national election in sight, the worried Democratic Administration moved to counter the political blows it was receiving. Loyalty procedures were instituted that, at the very best, were questionable, since they ignored the rights of the individual citizen. A rising hysteria took hold of America, and people saw enemies in strange places.

In Wheeling, West Virginia, it was discovered that candy sold to children had short geography lessons attached; one of these indicated that the Soviet Union was the largest nation on earth. The City Manager of Wheeling was shocked: "This is a terrible thing to expose our children to."

In Hollywood, plans to make a movie about poet Henry Wadsworth Longfellow were canceled. It had been revealed that Hiawatha, immortalized by Longfellow, had sought to settle disputes between warring Indian tribes by peaceful means, and this, a studio executive indicated, might be misunderstood as being part of the Communists' so-called peace offensive.

Counterattack, a magazine dedicated to extending Joe McCarthy's work, pointed out that Irene Wicker, an actress who portrayed the Singing Lady for children on television, had been listed by the *Daily Worker* as a sponsor of a left-wing candidate for the city council of New York. Said *Counterattack*, "The *Daily Worker* is very accurate; they never make a mistake." Miss Wicker's contract was ended.

The panic infested others. Men who owned supermarkets told radio and television networks whom they might employ and, if they failed to do so, certain advertised products were removed from the shelves. Sponsors, anxious to maintain sales, to offend no potential customer, joined the clamor.

A blacklist came into being in the entertainment business, extending from New York to Hollywood. Respected actors and directors were abruptly denied work, and there was no real way they could strike back, since no one would admit the existence of the illegal blacklist. Some very talented people abandoned their chosen professions. Others left the country, found work in England, Italy, Greece. A few simply died, some at their own hands. For blacklisted writers it was easier. They continued to write scripts, but under assumed names, and the producers continued to buy their work—for vastly diminished fees, of course.

In Washington, Robert Taft, staunch defender of the constitutional way, was able to make a remarkable statement: that the President had the temerity to "assume the innocence of all the persons mentioned in the State Department." He also said, "Whether Senator McCarthy has legal evidence, whether he has overstated or understated his case, is of lesser importance. The question is whether the Communist influence in the State Department still exists."

But not everyone in government took McCarthy's wild charges with such equanimity. Senator William Benton of Connecticut, outraged by the attack on General George Marshall, demanded Senator McCarthy's expulsion, leveling ten specific charges at him from the Senate floor. They included perjury, fraud, deceit and lack of fitness for office. The Benton resolution was turned over to the Rules Committee for investigation. Only one witness testified in public session—Senator Benton. McCarthy refused to testify or to make a direct response of any kind, but he did write a letter to Senator Guy M. Gillette, chairman of the Committee: "Frankly, Guy, I have not and do not intend to even read, much less answer, Benton's smear attack. I am sure you realize that the Benton type of material can be found in the *Daily Worker* almost any day of the week and will continue to flow from the mouths and pens of the campfollowers as long as I continue my attack against Communists in government."

There was McCarthy at work—when attacked, strike back. Charged with fraud and perjury, he suggested a connection between Benton and the Communists. In a typical performance, he muddied the waters, befogged the air, piled up charges and countercharges.

Nor did he stop there. McCarthy eventually attacked Chairman Gillette so fiercely that Gillette chose to resign from the committee. McCarthy demanded and obtained the personnel files of the committee's staff members, the implication being that he was going to expose their "Communist" backgrounds. Two members resigned just prior to the September primary in Wisconsin, in which McCarthy was a candidate, claiming an anti-McCarthy plot hatched by the Democratic members of the committee.

Much later, when the report of the investigation was at last made public, it proved to be a masterwork of moral paralysis, taking no stand: "The committee itself is not making any recommendations in this matter. The record should speak for itself. The issue raised is one for the entire Senate. . . ."

Joe McCarthy was a big man at the Republican National Convention of 1952. He was introduced as Wisconsin's Fighting Marine, the man who was "exposing the traitors in our government." When he spoke, he termed Douglas MacArthur "the greatest American that was ever born" and insisted that President Truman took the United States into Korea for publicity purposes. On the morning after the convention chose General Dwight David Eisenhower as its nominee for President, McCarthy provided his opinion of the party ticket. "I think Dick Nixon will make a fine Vice President," he said.

This lack of enthusiasm for Eisenhower didn't keep the Senator from campaigning for the general. He went on television to attack the Democratic candidate, Adlai E. Stevenson, in a series of allegations and implications, using guilt by association, suggesting evidence that was nonexistent.

"Tonight," he began, "I shall give you the history of the Democrat candidate . . . who endorses and would continue the suicidal Kremlin-shaped policies of this nation. . . . Stevenson's biography . . . states that [Archibald] MacLeish was the man who brought him into the State Department. MacLeish has been affiliated with . . . Communist-fronts. . . . Alger Hiss and Frank Coe recommended Adlai Stevenson as a delegate to a conference which was to determine our post-war policy in Asia. . . . I hold in my hand the official record of the series of lectures . . .

"I want to show you a picture of the barn . . .

"Now let's look at the photostat . . .

"I hold in my hand copies . . .

"The Democrat candidate made a statement that I had not convicted a single Communist. . . . While his statement is technically correct, its implication is viciously untrue. . . . I am neither a judge nor a jury nor a prosecutor. . . .

"I hold in my hand . . .

"I hold in my hand . . .

"We must have a Republican administration . . . and Congress. . . . We will have the power to help Dwight Eisenhower scrub and flush and wash clean the foul mess of corruption and Communism in Washington."

One of the most devastating aspects of McCarthyism was that it caused otherwise honorable men to compromise their ideals. It weakened their resolve, frightened them. During the campaign of 1952, General Eisenhower appeared in Wisconsin on the same platform with McCarthy, ready to include in his speech a powerful defense of his former colleague, George Marshall. But Eisenhower's advisers were fearful of McCarthy's reaction and advised him against praising Marshall. The Senator himself made no effort to censor Eisenhower's speech. In the end Eisenhower put personal loyalty and integrity aside and made no comment that might unsettle McCarthy.

On election day, Joe McCarthy was an easy winner; his critic, William Benton, was overwhelmingly defeated in his home state of Connecticut, and Dwight D. Eisenhower became President of the United States. McCarthy hailed the change the next day: "Now it will be unnecessary for me to conduct a one-man campaign to expose Communists in government. We have a new President who doesn't want party-line thinkers or fellow travelers. He will conduct the fight." Yet within a month McCarthy was saying again, "We've only scratched the surface on Communism." Senator Taft had other ideas. He expected to control McCarthy, to steer his activities into less sensitive areas. It was planned to continue the anti-Communist hunt, of course, but under the direction of Senator William Jenner, new chairman of the Senate Internal Security Committee, and Representative Harold Velde, who headed the House Committee on un-American Activities. Under a Republican Administration, it was expected, McCarthy would do little harm, attract little attention.

Taft could not have been more wrong. McCarthy had come to public attention by stirring political waters, and he intended to continue doing so.

In July, 1953, Senator Taft died. Joe McCarthy, however, was alive and well in the Senate, seeking the path to continued self-exploitation. It was inevitable that he find it.

Shortly after his election, Dwight Eisenhower fulfilled a campaign promise by going to Korea. He looked around, talked to some officers and enlisted men, and returned to the United States in order to form his own government and prepare for his inauguration.

Once in office, the new Administration set to work in accordance with the conservative policies so often enunciated by Robert Taft. Federal construction was diminished. Fewer people were hired for government work. Wage and price controls were eliminated. Offshore oil deposits were placed under control of the states, resulting in larger profits for the big oil firms. The head of the National Bureau of Standards, which examined and tested many of the products of private enterprise, was abruptly fired, a victim evidently of a job done too well. [Later he was quietly reinstated.] Rigid farm supports were replaced by more flexible ones, and the chairman of the Commission on Inter-Governmental Relations recommended that the Tennessee Valley Authority, supplier of cheap electricity to that area, be sold to private utility companies.

Then an event drew all eyes to Moscow. Joseph Stalin, dictator and tyrant, for so many years ruler of the Soviet Union, died. Georgi Malenkov became the new Premier of the U. S. S. R. An era had ended, but no one could tell what lay ahead.

In Korea, a shaky truce, begun under the Truman Administration, continued while peace negotiations went on.

In East Berlin, there were riots against the Communist regime.

And in the United States, the execution of the atom spies, Julius and Ethel Rosenberg, was stayed, temporarily.

Finally, on July 28, in the little building at Panmunjom, Korea, where negotiations had been conducted, a truce agreement was signed. After thirty-seven months and two days, the fighting which had claimed the lives of 33,461 Americans, plus 115,000 other casualties, which cost $22 billion, the war which had never been labeled a war was over.

The North Koreans were back behind the thirty-eighth parallel, and the troops of the Republic of Korea settled south of that line. Aggression had been halted, proved unprofitable, as Harry Truman had intended. It was a peace Truman would have made gladly, but one the American people might not have accepted while he was Commander-in-Chief, largely because of the attacks of Joe McCarthy against his Administration.

All that was changed now. Harry Truman was retired to Independence, Missouri, and Republicans ruled the Congress, sat in the White House. Joe McCarthy was their inheritance—and their problem.

XI

THE GRAND TOUR OF COHN AND SCHINE

WITH THE PRESSURES OF KOREA REMOVED, EISENHOWER WAS free to pursue policies that differed from the preceding Administration. Containment of world Communism, and its growing costs, constant concern with the opinions of our allies, financial support for countries that frequently refused to act in a fashion to our liking—these things jarred Republican global thinkers. Republican Party policy was rooted in a tight economic base and in rejecting the alarming idea that a world revolution was in progress. Sadly, this inability to perceive the changes taking place around the world did not eliminate them.

Secretary of State John Foster Dulles warned that failure to produce "political, economic and military unity" in Western Europe would "compel an agonizing reappraisal of basic United States policy." Later he spoke of "the further deterrent of massive retaliatory power. A potential aggressor must know that he cannot always prescribe battle conditions that suit him. . . ."

Both he and the President warned that America would use tactical atomic weaponry should a general war break out in Asia. The President said, "In any combat where these things can be used on strictly military targets and have strictly military purposes, I see no reason why they should not be used just exactly as you would use a bullet or anything else. . . ."

This drew immediate and contrary reactions. Adlai Stevenson suggested that the Administration was placing dollars ahead of security and the unity of the Western nations. And General Matthew Ridgway, a member of the Joint Chiefs, argued against economies, against current plans for reducing the size of United States ground forces.

At the heart of the Administration's stance was the abandonment of the containment policy, coupled with a warning to the Communist nations to behave "or else." Secretary of State Dulles went further than this. He was for a policy of liberating the countries under Communist domination, but he did not make clear how this was to be done.

Of the increasingly complex and unruly times in which problems refused to be settled by simplistic means, in which nations refused to be intimidated, Secretary Dulles said, "What we need to do is to recapture the kind of crusading spirit of the early days of the Republic when we were certain that we had something better than anyone else and we knew the rest of the world needed it and wanted it and that we were going to carry it around the world."

But those days had long passed into history. The world had been altered radically and was destined to change even more. Men and nations were no longer satisfied with life as it was, were imbued with rising expectations. Failure to recognize and to deal with this new reality could only make matters worse.

One result of the Republican triumph in the 1952 elections

was to place Joe McCarthy in charge of a committee of his own—the Permanent Subcommittee on Investigations of the Committee on Government Operations. Instead of his stature being diminished, as Taft had intended, McCarthy was a large and thoroughly intimidating figure on the political landscape.

It was generally held that eight Senators owed their seats to McCarthy's efforts on their behalf. And added to this was a widespread and very vocal support for the Senator across America.

With the new President anxious to avoid any public confrontation with McCarthy and equally anxious to maintain party unity, McCarthy seemed to have license to lump all his displeasures into a single bag—anti-Communism. He was a force to be reckoned with, his strength real and unrivaled. He was at the apex of his power.

He wasted no time making his intentions known. Even as the new Administration got under way, McCarthy announced that he knew there were still Communists in the State Department. Secretary Dulles, he suggested, would do well to get a security officer able to clean house. Dulles responded by naming Scott McLeod to this post. McLeod was generally assumed to be McCarthy's man.

In March, McCarthy made a startling announcement. He had, he said, managed to get Greek shippers to stop trading in Communist ports. An immediate uproar resulted. Here was blatant Senatorial interference in the business of the Executive Branch of the government, something expressly forbidden by the constitutional separation of powers. Eisenhower wanted the matter settled quickly and quietly, so John Foster Dulles and McCarthy had lunch together. Later, the President publicly suggested that the Senator might have made a "mistake."

But McCarthy's biggest mistake was still to come. Ironically it came out of his newfound power. Previously he had worked virtually alone, freewheeling, depending on his own aggressiveness and his flair for making headlines, his ability to confuse and confound, to misdirect attention from his errors. Things were different now, however. For his committee McCarthy required a staff, and he hired one. Among others, there were Francis D. Flanagan, general counsel, and his young assistant, Robert F. Kennedy. Mainly, though, there was Roy Cohn—twenty-five years old, as aggressive as McCarthy himself, glib, shrewd, arrogant—named to be chief counsel to the Subcommittee on Investigations.

Cohn was the son of a New York judge, who was a power in local Democratic politics. At twenty, Roy Cohn had compiled an enviable academic record, attending such fine schools as Fieldston, Horace Mann and Columbia University. He was admitted to the New York bar at twenty-one and joined the staff of the United States Attorney, working on smuggling and narcotics cases. Eventually he directed his attention to the Communist cause. He played a role in the case against the Rosenbergs, in the case against thirteen Communists accused of conspiring to overthrow the government and in the perjury indictment brought against Owen Lattimore (an indictment later dismissed and then withdrawn).

Once established, Cohn brought to the McCarthy committee, as an "unpaid consultant" on Communism, G. David Schine, a close friend of his, member of a family which owned a chain of hotels and movie theaters. Schine, at twenty-six, tall and good looking, had once done publicity work for an orchestra leader, had himself written a few songs. But it was a six-page paper called "Definition of Communism," generously distributed throughout the family hotel chain, which, according to Roy Cohn, gave Schine value to the committee.

This representation of Schine's expertise concerning Communism was somewhat less than perfect in its scholarship. It managed, for example, to place the Russian Revolution, as well

A Baltimore auto dealer erected this monument dedicated to Senator McCarthy in front of his place of business. Someone obviously disagreed.

Pussyfootprints On The Sands Of Time
8/3/1954

from Herblock's Here and Now *(Simon & Schuster, 1955).*

The 36 volumes of the Army-McCarthy Hearings, one for each day.

Special Senate Committee that investigated censure charges against Senator Joseph R. McCarthy, left to right: Senators Frank Carlson, John C. Stennis, Arthur Watkins (Chairman), Edwin C. Johnson, Francis Case, Samuel Ervin.

12/3/1954

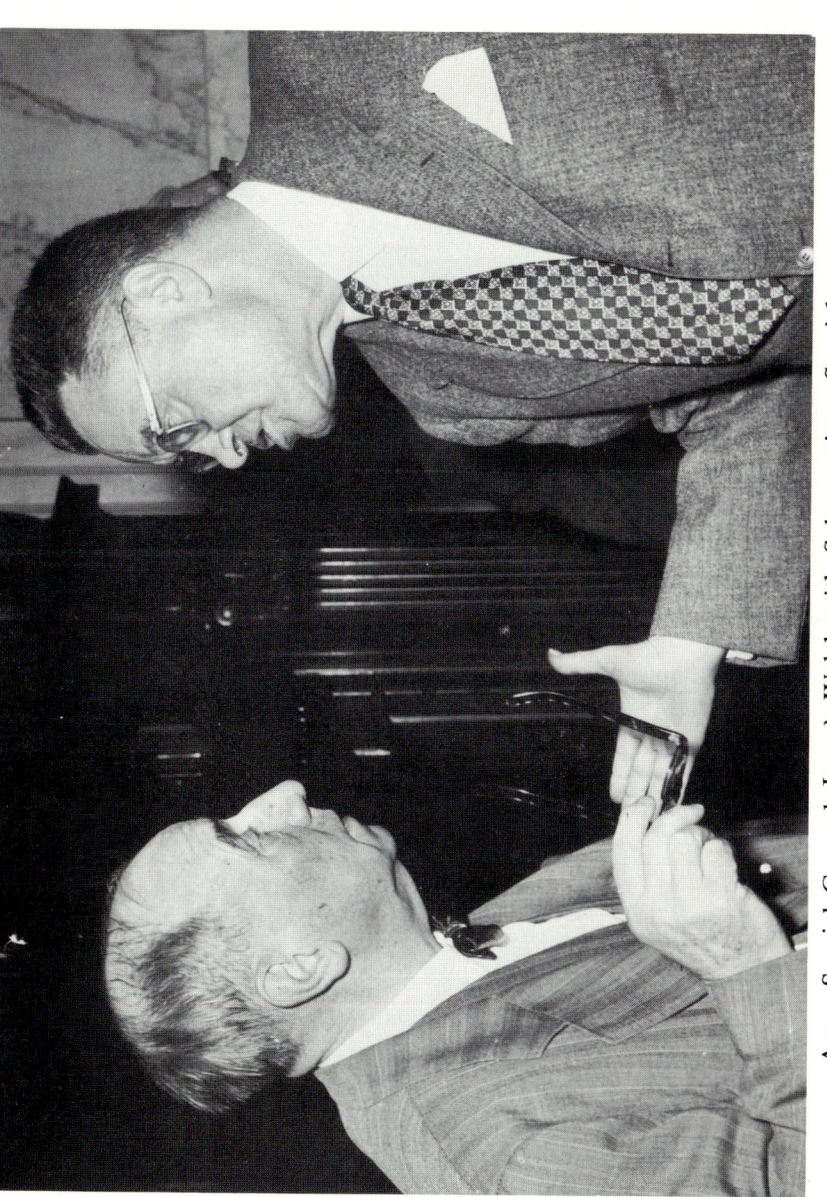

Army Special Counsel Joseph Welch with Subcommittee Special Counsel Ray Jenkins.

"I Pledge Allegiance To Joe McCarthy
And To The Committee Which Stands For Him—"
6/17/1954

from Herblock's Here and Now *(Simon & Schuster, 1955).*

"We Killed 'Em
In Europe, Boss"
4/23/1953

from Herblock's Here and Now *(Simon & Schuster, 1955).*

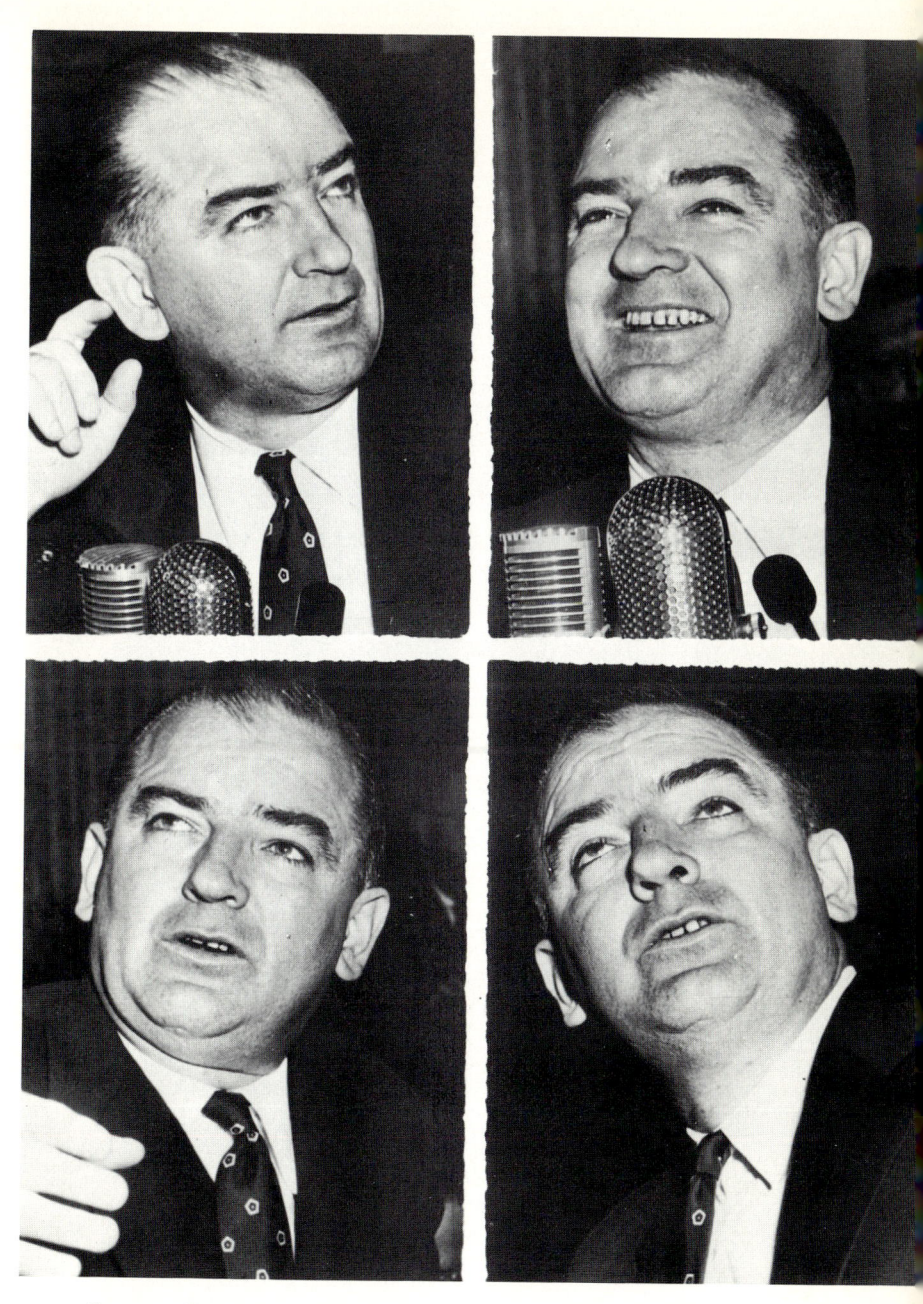

Senator Joseph R. McCarthy at the Army-McCarthy Hearings, February 26, 1954.

Senator McCarthy with G. David Schine and Roy Cohn.

"I Have Here In My Hand—"
5/7/1954
from Herblock's Here And Now *(Simon & Schuster, 1955)*.

as the founding of the Communist Party and the first of Russia's Five Year Plans in the wrong years. In his paper Schine also confused Alexander Kerensky with Prince Lvov, Joseph Stalin with Leon Trotsky, Marx with Lenin, and he gave Lenin the wrong first name.

This flawed primer had brought David Schine to the attention of columnist George Sokolsky who introduced him to Roy Cohn. The two young men became friends. Recruiting them for his committee must have seemed like a coup to Senator McCarthy at the time, but he was wrong. Roy Cohn and David Schine were to be Joe McCarthy's biggest tactical error.

The McCarthy Committee, as it came to be known, announced various investigations—of the Government Printing Office, defense plants, the Voice of America, the Federal scholarship and the academic-exchange programs, as well as others.

One investigation McCarthy proposed was to focus on the Central Intelligence Agency. But an open investigation of that highly sensitive body would inevitably do damage to American security, and the Administration made that clear to McCarthy; he dropped the idea.

In his book *McCarthy,* Roy Cohn referred to this abortive effort: "Thus it remained for a muckraking magazine published by young West Coast radicals to expose in sensational fashion the CIA's soiled linen to an astonished public—fourteen years after Joe McCarthy had been denied access to this holiest of holies." He failed to say that the magazine, *Ramparts,* took great glee in exposing the CIA's involvement in private industry and in the colleges and universities of America, using them to fight *against* Communism domestically and abroad.

Like McCarthy himself, Roy Cohn would not be denied his place in the sun. It really began in April, 1953, when he and David Schine embarked on a journey that landed them on front pages around the world. They would seldom enjoy anonymity again. Their jet-paced tour took them to eighteen European cities, in each of which they intended to ferret out Communist influence and subversion in the State Department's overseas information program. In *McCarthy,* Roy Cohn described the program this way:

> The information program that caused such bitter controversy consisted of American libraries and reading rooms set up in foreign countries. They weren't intended to function as public or general libraries but to house reading matter about our country, its people, and their way of life. They were Cold War products whose purpose was to win friends.

What Cohn neglected to say is that one of the strengths, and most attractive aspects of life in America, is the diversity of that life, the freedom of speech, spoken or written, the freedom to read whatever one may choose to read, to explore different and conflicting ideas, to dissent. A view of America that fails to demonstrate this fundamental fact of our political existence is necessarily a false one. The same was, of course, true in 1953.

Cohn and Schine began their search for orthodoxy in Paris, spending some forty hours in that city. There, according to Cohn, they discovered that a certain amount of duplication of work resulted in a waste of taxpayers' money. Government work being what it is, such revelations could have been made in Washington with equal accuracy.

Next, they went to Frankfurt, Germany, for nineteen hours; spent twenty hours in Berlin, sixteen hours in Bonn, sixty in Munich, forty-one in Vienna, twenty-three in Belgrade, twenty-four hours in Athens, twenty more in Rome and just six hours in London.

In Bonn, Cohn and Schine stated they were hunting for subversives.

In Paris, they said they were out to eliminate inefficiency in government.

In Munich, Cohn claimed to be looking for both, the subversive and the inefficient.

In Rome, informed that Senator McCarthy had suggested they were trying to find out how much money had been spent "putting across the Truman Administration," Cohn confessed that "we haven't heard about that but anything the chairman of our committee says, if he said it, goes with us."

In Vienna, Cohn told everyone that he had no information about American subversion in Austria. However, Schine and he did tour the Soviet Information Center where they managed to find works of the American authors Theodore Dreiser and Mark Twain, who could be discovered in libraries all over the world, to the credit of the United States. They spent less than another thirty minutes inspecting the American library. Satisfied at last, they flew home.

Though the trip and its consequences were no joke, it resembled some theatrical farce brought into the streets. Trailed everywhere by a small army of newspapermen, Cohn and Schine were arrogant, often flippant, and indulged in vulgar jokes. The excursion drew the kind of attention generally reserved only for the scandals of movie stars, all under the guise of representing the best interests of the United States of America.

To help them in their work, Cohn and Schine employed a woman named Hede Massing, formerly the wife of Gerhart Eisler, a Russian spy, and herself a former Communist agent, and Hermann Aumer, an unemployed German politician who had lost his seat in the Bundestag when it was revealed that he had been given 22,000 marks by a petroleum company to influence him to vote for a hike in gasoline prices.

Critics abroad and at home charged the trip had served only to make America a laughingstock and brought morale in government agencies to a new low. Several employees resigned, including Theodore Kaghan, Public Affairs Officer in the United States High Commission for Germany. Kaghan, it seemed, had once shared an apartment with a Communist, but apparently his major error was to describe Cohn and Schine as "junketeering gumshoes."

The State Department's reaction to the quick inspection was to ban the "books, music, paintings . . . of any Communists, fellow traveler, et cetera." That so amorphous "et cetera" allowed nervous librarians to remove the works of respected American writers, some of whom were known for their constructively militant anti-Communism.

Of this period, President Eisenhower told students at Dartmouth University:

> Don't join the book burners. Don't think you are going to conceal faults by concealing evidence that they ever existed. Don't be afraid to go in your library and read every book as long as any document does not offend our own ideas of decency. That should be the only censorship.
>
> How will we defeat communism unless we know what it is? what it teaches—why does it have such an appeal for men? . . . We've got to fight it with something better. Do not try to conceal the thinking of our own people. They are part of America and even if they think ideas that are contrary to ours they have a right to have them, a right to record them and a right to have them in places where they are accessible to others. It is unquestioned or it is not America.

Nevertheless Eisenhower was still concerned with party amity. While insisting he was against the suppression of ideas, against the burning of books, against censorship, he would offer no criticism of Senator McCarthy, his methods of intimidation or his aides. As if to underscore this ambivalence, Secretary Dulles remarked that only a small number of books had actually been destroyed.

Years later, when he was no longer the President, General Eisenhower stated that at the time he concluded that the best way he personally could treat McCarthy was to ignore him and not add to the flood of publicity that the Senator generated.

The specter of McCarthyism settled across the land. A member of the Indiana State Textbook Commission charged that there was a "Communist directive in education now to stress the story of Robin Hood. They want to stress it because he robbed the rich and gave it to the poor. That's the Communist line."

A play-writing contest was conducted by publisher Samuel French, in which the right was reserved "to declare ineligible any author who is, or becomes publicly involved, in a scholastic, literary, political, or moral controversy."

The drive for political orthodoxy was so strong in academic circles that Albert Einstein was constrained to advise teachers and scientists to refuse to testify before Congressional committees and accept jail sentences if necessary.

A handful of former diplomats issued a warning that attacks on the State Department were having "sinister results. . . . A premium has been put upon reporting and upon recommendations which are ambiguously stated or so cautiously set forth as to be deceiving. . . . The ultimate result is a threat to national security."

That threat hardly troubled Senator McCarthy. He was hot on the trail of a much greater danger to the national security— an anonymous Army dentist.

XII

A PINK ARMY DENTIST

IRVING PERESS WAS A BALDING MAN OF NO PARTICULAR DISTINCtion who practiced dentistry in the borough of Queens, in New York City. Under the Doctors Draft Act of 1950, he accepted a reserve commission as a captain in the Army. Like every member of the Armed Services, past and present, Peress filled out a profusion of official forms, supplying professional and personal data. One such form contained the following clause:

> I am not, nor have I been, a conscientious objector and I am not now and have not been a member of any foreign or domestic organization, association, movements, group, or combination of persons advocating a subversive policy or seeking to alter the form of government of the United States by unconstitutional means.

Peress signed the clause. Subsequently, however, when similar queries were put to him, he invoked the Fifth Amendment of the Constitution, which protects an individual against possible self-incrimination. This lawful act by an obscure dentist was to split opinion in the United States and bring the Army into direct conflict with Senator Joe McCarthy.

Peress, scheduled to be sent overseas, was informed that his wife, long a sufferer from an anxiety neurosis, had undergone a relapse. At the same time, his daughter was receiving treatment at a New York hospital. Peress asked for and received emergency leave. He also requested cancellation of his foreign assignment. This was granted, and he was stationed at Camp Kilmer, New Jersey.

While this was going on, the file on Peress had come into the intelligence division of the First Army in New York. Like thousands of other such files, it was flagged for further investigation. But the Army, smothering under tons of paperwork, of echelons of responsibilities, of reports and questionnaires in duplicate and triplicate, moved in its typically slow and often confounding way. As a result, it took more than three months for Intelligence even to locate Peress in Camp Kilmer, only thirty miles away.

Peress remained at Kilmer but his file traveled to the Disposition Section of G-2 in Washington, made its way leisurely through the stacks of similar files piled on desk after desk until it was sent on to Camp Kilmer. Someone had finally remembered that regulations demanded that the file proceed through regular channels at that base.

Three weeks later, the file was shipped back to Washington with the recommendation that "the retention of Peress in service was not consistent with the interest of national security because the investigation provided sufficient evidence to find that he had subversive tendencies."

Within the month, the Peress file had collected four recommendations that he be separated from the Army. Two came from

FREEDOM IN JEOPARDY

First Army, another from the intelligence officer at Camp Kilmer, the last one from the Office of the Surgeon General. Questionnaires were forwarded to Peress concerning any possible involvement on his part in subversive groups, and once again he invoked the Fifth Amendment. By this time, three additional recommendations had been made that he be returned to civilian life.

The peripatetic Peress file continued to work its way upward through the maze of security procedures. On October 21, Brigadier General Ralph W. Zwicker, commanding officer at Camp Kilmer, detailed the case against Peress to First Army Headquarters, and recommended that he be immediately relieved from duty.

While this was going on, other forces were at work. In September, the Congress amended the Doctors Draft Act so that dentists with experience equal to that accumulated by Irving Peress could be commissioned majors instead of captains. Peress, among many others, quite naturally wanted the higher rank and its attendant increase in pay.

To deal with the amendment to the act, the Defense Department created a committee to adjust the rank of medical officers. The basis for that adjustment was to be on strictly professional grounds. In due course, Irving Peress qualified under the new regulations and was automatically promoted to the rank of major.

In January of the new year, the Army, in line with the recommendations of its security officers, ordered Major Peress relieved from active duty and given an honorable discharge. Advised of this by General Zwicker, Peress (as was his privilege) chose March 31 for his discharge.

Before that could happen, however, Irving Peress was summoned to appear before the McCarthy Committee. Peress responded to questions by claiming the protection of the Fifth Amendment.

With this experience behind him, Peress had second thoughts about waiting until the end of March to receive his discharge.

He asked for it at once and was separated from the Army on the second of February.

Two weeks later he was back before the McCarthy Committee.

"Who signed your discharge?" the Senator wanted to know.

"John J. McManus, Major, Infantry," Peress replied.

"Where is John J. McManus located?"

"I have no idea."

At this point, McCarthy launched a rambling statement laced with undocumented charges and allegations, the kind of statement that caused so many people to label him more of a threat to liberty in America than were the persons he attacked.

"Let us have the record show," the Senator began, "that this was signed and handed to this Fifth Amendment Communist, Major Peress, after I had written the Secretary of the Army suggesting that he be court-martialed, suggesting that everyone having anything to do with his promotion, with his change of orders, be court-martialed. I did that feeling that this would be one way to notify all the officers in the Army that there has been a new day in the Army, that the twenty years of treason have ended and that no officer in the Army can protect traitors, can protect Communists."

Labeling Peress a Communist behind the immunity of the Senate was one thing; proving it was another. True, Peress had been "named" as a Communist by a policewoman acting as an undercover agent, but no evidence had been presented that would stand up in a court of law.

The phrase "Fifth Amendment Communist," a favored phrase of McCarthy's, implied that anyone using the Fifth Amendment was necessarily guilty of something; and that the Constitutional privilege itself was in some way to blame for offering a shield to those who would undermine the nation. Years later Supreme Court Justice Hugo Black would address himself to the controversy which has surrounded this provision: "I subscribe to the doctrine that the Fifth Amendment, which says, 'No person shall be compelled to be a witness against himself,' means that no person shall be compelled to be a witness against himself." It is a concept that eluded those who find something unsavory in that use of the Constitution.

As for McCarthy's recommendation of court-martial for those who had anything to do with Peress, that could have included the Senator himself, since his affirmative vote on the amendment to the Doctors Draft Act had helped bring about the dentist's promotion.

During Peress's appearance before his committee, McCarthy delivered a lengthy, disjointed diatribe at John Adams, legal counsel for the Army. McCarthy accused Peress of swearing he was not a member of the Communist Party (Peress had not so sworn), of refusing to answer the committee's questions (which was Peress's privilege under the Constitution), of acting in a manner unbecoming an officer (hardly the Senator's concern). McCarthy tossed around threats of court-martial (which was certainly far outside his authority), extending these to civilians and members of the Red Cross as well as to military personnel. He insisted that Peress was a Communist (which had yet to be established), rambled on about infiltration of the armed services (Peress had been drafted into the Army), described the dentist as "an important member of the Communist conspiracy." McCarthy then went on to threaten with a citation for contempt "any man in the military—and I do not care whether he is a civilian or an officer. . . ." He spoke of double-talk on the part of those concerned, of making an example of someone, and finally jerked his attention back to the dentist.

"Mr. Peress, while you were an officer in the Army, did you ever have access to any decoding or encoding machines?"

Peress, more accustomed to X-ray systems and dental drills, replied, "I don't even know what they are."

The Peress matter, and McCarthy's methods, began to disturb an increasing number of people in Washington. Republican Senator Ralph Flanders of Vermont subsequently rose in the Senate to accuse McCarthy of trying to shatter their party. McCarthy, Flanders said, "dons his war paint. He goes into his war dance. He emits his war whoops. He goes forth to battle and proudly returns with the scalp of a pink Army dentist. We may assume that this represents the depth of the seriousness of Communist penetration at this time."

Finished with Peress, but not with the Army, McCarthy called on General Ralph Zwicker to testify. Roy Cohn launched the questioning. He suggested that, regardless of what had gone on in relation to Peress, the charge of Communist activity would do no injury to Zwicker or others at Camp Kilmer. Zwicker agreed to that. McCarthy did not.

He interrupted. "It would reflect unfavorably upon some of them of course?"

Zwicker said he couldn't give an answer to that. McCarthy persisted. Surely Zwicker knew that someone had kept Peress in the Army knowing that he was a Communist? Zwicker replied that he did not know that to be a fact.

Dissatisfied with the answers he was getting, McCarthy blurted out, "General, let's try and be truthful. I am going to keep you here as long as you keep hedging and hemming."

"I am not hedging," Zwicker replied stiffly, displaying the control instilled in him at West Point.

"Or hawing."

"I don't like to have anyone impugn my honesty, which you just about did."

McCarthy bit off words angrily: "Either your honesty or your intelligence. I can't help impugning one or the other, when you tell us that a major in your command was known to you to have been before a Senate committee, and of whom you read the press releases very carefully—to now have you sit there and tell us that you did not know whether he refused to answer questions about Communist activities."

Zwicker replied formally: "Any information that appeared or any releases were well known to me and well known to plenty of other people long prior to the time that you ever called this man for investigation. And there were no facts or allegations— nothing presented from the time that he appeared before your first investigation—that was not apparent prior to that time."

There it was. The Army, in its own ponderous way, had been dealing with Peress, and others like him, long before McCarthy, or his aides, had become involved or interested in the matter. However, as the Army saw it, there had been no evidence on which to prosecute Peress; had there been, he would have been brought to trial.

The Senator wanted to know if Zwicker considered it proper to present an honorable discharge to a man known to be a Communist? Zwicker said he did not, but "anything that I am ordered to do by higher authority, I must accept."

The exchange went on, and when Zwicker's answers continued to displease McCarthy, the Senator's heavy-boned face turned crimson, and his voice climbed. "Then, General, you should be removed from any command. Any man who has been given the honor of being promoted to general and who says, 'I will protect another general who protected Communists' is not fit to wear that uniform. . . ."

Not fit to wear that uniform!

Ralph Zwicker was a colonel when he led his regiment ashore in the first wave at the Normandy invasion during World War II. For his actions that morning, he was awarded the Silver Star. He led his regiment south, and for his actions on August 1 he was decorated by Great Britain with the Distinguished Service

Cross. Later, that same month, Zwicker was awarded two of the three Bronze Stars he would eventually receive. For his efforts in defending the town of Elsenborn during the deadly Battle of the Bulge, he received the Legion of Merit. Clearly, Ralph Zwicker wore his uniform with distinction.

It was that uniform, and the uniform worn by an ordinary army private, that would combine to plague Joe McCarthy, to raise a national furor, to present a true picture of Tail Gunner Joe in action to the American people.

XIII

THE PRIVATE
AND THE SENATOR

No one was shooting at American soldiers or sailors or marines during the summer of 1953. But still the uniformed services were performing valuable duty around the world, posted in potential trouble spots, standing against further advances of the Soviet Union in Europe and in Asia. Each month men were drafted into the services, whether they chose to go or not, men with neither influence nor connections in high places, men who performed their duty as demanded by their country. Two World Wars had been fought by such men, and they had turned back the Chinese in Korea. In later years such men would fight in Vietnam. The risks were fewer in 1953, but the duty was no less vital.

Roy Cohn's close friend, G. David Schine, unpaid consultant to the McCarthy Committee, had been classified 4-F, due to a slipped disk. Now he was reexamined and reclassified, ordered to report for induction. In July, Major General Miles Reber, chief of Army Legislative Liaison, was summoned to Senator McCarthy's office. McCarthy told the general that he wanted David Schine to receive a direct commission. Roy Cohn added his voice, insisting the commission be made with all possible dispatch.

McCarthy's concern at this point was undoubtedly less impassioned than was Roy Cohn's. Subsequently, when Schine was actually in uniform, Cohn made an attempt to get him assigned back to the McCarthy Committee. At that point, McCarthy telephoned Secretary of the Army Robert Stevens, saying, "I would like to ask you one personal favor. For God's sake, don't put Dave in service and assign him back on my committee. . . . He is a good boy, but there is nothing indispensable about him. . . . It is one of the few things I have seen Roy completely unreasonable about. . . ."

During this period, McCarthy began an investigation of an alleged espionage plot at the Army Signal Corps Radar Center at Fort Monmouth. Here again, there was considerable bombast and fuss on the part of McCarthy, while little or nothing that had not been previously known was uncovered. Instead, there was disruption of routines, and the sensitive work being done at Fort Monmouth was slowed, made more difficult. In the words of President Eisenhower, "After a long, drawn-out and dreary investigation, the charge collapsed completely."

This was reflected in the report of the subcommittee of the Federation of American Scientists, which reviewed the charges. It was discovered that one man was accused of belonging to the Young Pioneers of America back in 1933. The source of another's troubles was a meeting he had once attended at which a lecture on Israel had been given. A third man was a member of a veterans' organization to which the President of the United States also belonged. The subcommittee report stated, "Of over 120 charges against nineteen employees which were analyzed in detail, only six involved Communist membership or affiliations, five of which were denied under oath; the sixth was an admission of attending Communist meetings with the employee's mother at the age of twelve or thirteen."

Many of the accused, simply because they had been accused, suffered acutely. Neighbors stopped talking to them, refuse was deposited on their lawns and porches, their children were beaten up by other children, car pools rejected otherwise acceptable riders. That was the patriotic harvest reaped at Fort Monmouth.

Meanwhile, Roy Cohn was not having much success in his efforts to keep David Schine out of the Army. Nor had he been able to obtain a direct commission for him. Though draft deferments and direct commissions were not impossible to obtain for those with the right connections, Schine's close link with the McCarthy Committee made his situation more delicate. If his commissioning were too blatant, too obviously a question of favoritism, and it became public knowledge, there would ensue a very bad public reaction.

As for Schine himself, he suffered from no false modesty. He suggested to Secretary of the Army Stevens that he, Schine, might become his special assistant instead of just another soldier. The Secretary failed to respond to this idea, and Schine was eventually drafted, and became a member of K company at Fort Dix, New Jersey.

But David Schine became no ordinary soldier. During his stay at Fort Dix, he managed to make or receive some 250 telephone calls, and was frequently released from formations in order to do so. He was allowed passes on all weekends and holidays, far from normal procedure for a rookie in basic training. One rainy day, with his company on the firing range, Schine was discovered huddled in a truck. He said he was studying logistics and other matters he considered relevant to reforming the Army along more modern lines. According to testimony given later by the Army,

Schine used his Washington connections to be excused from kitchen duty. Schine also let it be known that for him to sign out, as did other soldiers, when he left the post, would be rather "obvious"; and according to his commanding officer, he sought special favors from both commissioned and noncommissioned officers. He informed his company commander that he would mention him favorably in "reports" he was filing. And one morning he left Fort Dix without leave.

Despite the extraordinary behavior allowed Schine, Roy Cohn was not satisfied. Pressure from him and from Joe McCarthy on Private Schine's behalf increased. Cohn made a threat to "wreck the Army."

The Army was impelled to fight back. It released a report charging McCarthy and Cohn with making threats and using improper methods in order to obtain preferential treatment for Schine. This was spelled out in thirty-four detailed pages.

As usual, Senator McCarthy's defense was to attack—by charging that Secretary Stevens had tried to get him to investigate the Navy and the Air Force instead of the Army. He charged also that the Army's legal counsel, John Adams, had offered to reveal information about an air force base supposedly infested with homosexuals in exchange for advance information about the next army installation to be investigated by McCarthy's Committee. He further claimed that the Army was holding David Schine as a hostage in order to put an end to such investigations. He accused John Adams of saying he would fight the committee.

Obviously something was wrong.
Obviously someone was lying.
Obviously something had to be done.

Here was a situation that could only besmirch all parties to it. To prevent this, the Senate acted, hoping to mediate, to quiet the discord, to heal the public rift. It ordered an investigation.

It was decided that McCarthy's own subcommittee should

conduct the hearings, under a seven-man "special committee." McCarthy was to step down as chairman. All other committee matters were to be postponed while the charges and counter-charges were explored. An outside counsel and a new staff would be employed for this purpose.

What followed, and was seen via television, came to be known as the Army-McCarthy Hearings.

For the first time millions of people were able to see the Senator from Wisconsin in action over a prolonged period of time, to weigh his motives, his methods and his recklessness, to receive the full impact of his personality as he attacked the Army of the United States.

XIV

POINT OF ORDER

A MOMENTOUS YEAR, 1954.

It was the year America exploded the first hydrogen bomb, the most destructive weapon man had ever conceived. The existence of the bomb, many people claimed, could mean the end of the world. Or its salvation.

In March, Earl Warren, former governor of California, was named Chief Justice of the Supreme Court. The decisions of the so-called Warren Court would be a source of controversy throughout his service.

Later that spring, the Supreme Court in an historic decision declared school segregation unconstitutional, thus bringing the nation one step closer to true equality under the law.

In May, the French defenders at Dien Bien Phu in Indochina (now Vietnam) succumbed to the Vietminh under Ho Chi

Minh. Later, a truce would be signed, and for the first time in twenty-three years, there would be no shooting war anywhere in the world.

And on the morning of April 22, the Army-McCarthy Hearings got under way. Continuing for thirty-six days, they provided a public spectacle such as the United States had never before experienced. At times, more than twenty million people looked in on the televised happenings, reacting with fascination, horror and shame as the hearing that had been intended as an exercise in mediation became in fact a public political bloodletting.

Chairman of the Special Committee was Senator Karl Mundt of South Dakota. His fellow Republicans included Everett Dirksen of Illinois, Charles E. Potter of Michigan and Henry Dworshak of Idaho. The Democrats were John McClellan of Arkansas, Stuart Symington of Missouri and Henry Jackson of Washington.

Chairman Mundt gripped his pipe tightly as the red lights of the television cameras glowed, telling him that millions of voters were watching and listening. He rapped for silence.

It was the claim of the Army, Senator Mundt said, that Senator McCarthy, Roy Cohn and the McCarthy Committee's executive director, Francis Carr, had attempted to obtain preferential treatment for Private David Schine. The three men had, in turn, leveled forty-six charges against the Army, claiming an attempt to "force discontinuance of further attempts by that committee to expose Communist infiltration in the Army."

It was the purpose of the present investigation, Mundt went on, "to make a full and impartial effort to reveal that which is true and to expose that which is false with respect to the charges and the countercharges."

Senator Mundt would shortly discover that the proceedings were going to flood over into other areas and personalities, and issues not mentioned in the original charges would be introduced. In the battle about to begin, no holds were barred, and no rules existed that could not be broken. No charge could *not* be brought, however wild or unrelated to fact.

"It is our joint determination," Mundt said, "to conduct these hearings with a maximum degree of dignity, firmness and thoroughness. We enter our duties with no prejudgment as to the verities in this controversy. We propose to follow the evidence where it leads and to give every party to this dispute the equitable treatment and consideration to which he is entitled."

Joe McCarthy and Roy Cohn listened to none of this, their heads being together in whispered consultation.

Mundt introduced Senator John McClellan, senior Democrat on the committee, who offered a few words in behalf of fairness and impartiality and truth. There was no rebuttal.

Chairman Mundt turned to Ray H. Jenkins, counsel for the Special Committee. "Call the first witness."

Ray Jenkins was a craggy-faced conservative Republican from Tennessee, a man in his late fifties. An excellent criminal lawyer, he had compiled a lengthy record of courtroom victories. *The New York Times* described him as the sort of a lawyer "who completely dominates a case and a court. Rising with square jaw set and fire in his eyes, he'll unbutton his collar, loosen his coat, untie his tie and go to work. The gestures of his hands are almost as gripping as his oratory. He reminds one of a boxer dog when he sets his jaw. He laughs, cries, derides, always showing emotion." Now, ordered to summon the first witness, Ray Jenkins opened his mouth to speak a name.

The voice of Joe McCarthy was heard instead: "A point of order, Mr. Chairman; may I raise a point of order?"

It was the first of an uncountable number of such points of order that McCarthy was to raise. Under parliamentary practice, a point of order is, of course, intended only to question procedure or propriety under the rules of the matter immediately under discussion. It is not meant to be used, as McCarthy proceeded throughout the Army hearings to misuse it, to inhibit, to slow, to divert the hearings.

He spoke from behind lips that barely moved, in a flat drone, eyes downcast, swiveling his chair from side to side. "I have heard," he said, "from people in the military all the way from generals with the most upstanding combat records down to privates recently inducted, and they indicate they are very resentful of the fact that a few Pentagon politicians attempting to disrupt our investigations are naming themselves the Department of the Army. . . . The Department of the Army is not doing this. It is three civilians in the Army, and they should be so named."

These Pentagon politicians, McCarthy neglected to mention, were the highest officials in the military establishment, appointed by the President in keeping with the widely respected and honored tradition of maintaining civilian supremacy over the uniformed forces.

At last the first witness was called. He was Major General Miles Reber, commanding general, Western Area Command of the United States Army in Europe. The general, previously stationed at the Pentagon, had, in July and August of 1953, tried to get a commission for David Schine. He testified about this effort in a dispassionate manner, careful to exhibit no bias one way or another. Reber recalled that Roy Cohn had informed him at the time in question that David Schine had served as an officer in the Army Transport Service. In fact, Schine had been a purser and a civilian. Nothing more.

Under questioning by Senator Potter, General Reber said that neither McCarthy nor Cohn had intimidated or threatened him. He went on to say, however, that unusual pressure was put forth on Schine's behalf.

"It wasn't the normal action?" Potter asked.

"It was more than normal."

Eventually it was the chance of the army counsel, Joseph Welch, a Boston lawyer with a courtly manner and a drooping countenance. At sixty-three, Welch possessed an inner strength encased in a slight figure and a gentle manner. An Iowan by birth, he had made a brilliant record as a student at Harvard Law School and an equally brilliant record in the courtroom. He wasted no time on preliminaries with General Reber.

"Were you acutely aware of Mr. Cohn's position as counsel for this committee in the course of your conversation and contacts with him?"

"I was, Mr. Welch."

"Did that position occupied by Mr. Cohn increase or diminish the interest with which you pursued the problem?"

"To the best of my ability, I feel that it increased the interest."

"One more question, sir. Disregarding the word 'improper' influence or pressure, do you recall any instance comparable to this in which you were put under greater pressure?"

"To the best of my recollection, I recall of no instance under which I was put under greater pressure."

Here was a respected army officer testifying in a calm and impartial manner. Nothing he had done or said could be construed as hostile, but to Senator McCarthy, General Reber's very style must have seemed a threat; he was someone to be attacked, his credibility destroyed by any technique that would do the job.

"Is Sam Reber your brother?" Senator McCarthy asked, after a whispered exchange with Roy Cohn.

"Yes, sir."

Sam Reber had been the Acting High Commissioner for the State Department in Germany during the Cohn-Schine European trip.

"General," McCarthy said, "at the time that you were processing the application of this young man Schine for a commission, were you aware of the fact that he had had a very unpleasant experience with your brother, who was the Acting High Commissioner in Germany?"

General Reber had no knowledge of such an incident. But that didn't deter McCarthy. He plunged ahead, building a case entirely of his own making.

"Do you know that Mr. Sam Reber was the superior to Mr. [Theodore] Kaghan who Mr. Cohn and Mr. Schine were sent to Europe by me to inspect . . . that your brother, Mr. Sam Reber, repeatedly made attacks upon them and that your brother, Mr. Sam Reber, appointed a man to shadow them. . . . Were you aware of that at the time you were making this great effort to get consideration as you say for Mr. Schine?"

Sam Reber's "attacks," as McCarthy characterized them, had consisted only of his refusal to denounce Ted Kaghan as a "Communist sympathizer," since Kaghan had been in fact one of the most effective anti-Communist fighters then in Germany. As for the so-called "shadow" McCarthy mentioned, he was a member of the Visitors Bureau who had been assigned, at the request of Cohn and Schine, to arrange hotel reservations, plane schedules and other appointments for them.

None of these facts interfered with McCarthy's continued assault on General Reber by way of his brother. "Are you aware of the fact that your brother was allowed to resign when charges that he was a bad security risk were made against him as a result of the investigations of this committee?"

Ray Jenkins maintained that the question was irrelevant and so McCarthy restated it in even more damaging terms: "This question is of the utmost importance . . . if his brother was forced to resign . . . because he was a bad security risk. . . ."

Senator McClellan, demonstrating a concern for legal proprieties, objected: "There has been no testimony that the statements that the Senator makes as facts are true, and until they are established in this record as facts, then the question is incompetent. . . . Let us have a ruling on this because we may be trying members of everybody's family involved before we get through."

Joseph Welch wanted to know why Sam Reber had retired from the State Department and asked General Reber to answer. Before he could, Joe McCarthy broke in: "That is a completely unfair question!"

General Reber, visibly disturbed, tried to respond. "A very serious charge has been made against my brother in this room. I would like to answer publicly that charge right now."

After conferring with Chairman Mundt, Counsel Jenkins offered a startling assessment of what had transpired: "General Reber, I think, is in error in stating that a serious attack has been made on his brother. Suggestions were asked . . . but no proof or statement has been introduced. . . ."

Senator Jackson spoke up: "The statement, Mr. Chairman, has been made in this room and it is apparent to millions of Americans that General Reber's brother was dismissed as a security risk! . . . The statement cannot be stricken from all the newspapers tonight or from the television audience and radio audience, and I think in fairness he should be given the opportunity to answer the statement . . . that his brother was dismissed as a security risk."

The argument continued for two hours until Chairman Mundt ruled that General Reber could talk about his brother, despite Joe McCarthy's final objection.

The general spoke: "I merely wanted to say that, as I understand my brother's case, he retired—as he is entitled to do by law—upon reaching the age of fifty. That is all I wanted to say."

The facts were simple. Samuel Reber had never been charged with being a security risk. He had not been forced to resign.

After twenty-eight years in the Foreign Service, entitled to a pension, he had retired, three years after he was authorized to do so.

Secretary of the Army Robert Stevens was a former businessman accustomed to dealing with his fellows for mutual gain. In the naked jungle of Washington politics, he was out of his element.

When McCarthy and Roy Cohn decided to get a commission for David Schine, they had summoned Stevens to meet with them in Schine's plush suite in New York's Waldorf Towers. The next morning, Stevens rode down to the Foley Square courthouse to attend the McCarthy Committee's investigation of the Army in David Schine's Cadillac. When he was called to the witness stand during the Army-McCarthy Hearings, Stevens testified about that ride.

"Was anything said to you," Ray Jenkins wanted to know, "with reference to preferential treatment to be accorded Mr. Schine?"

"Well, Mr. Schine and I had quite an interesting talk in the car riding downtown."

"Will you relate what the conversation was? . . ."

"Well, the conversation was along the line that I was doing a good job ferreting out Communists."

"Was that your statement or his?"

"That was Mr. Schine's statement. . . . He thought I could go a long way in this field. And he would like to help me. He thought that it would be a much more logical plan for him to become a special assistant of mine."

"Than do what?" Jenkins pressed.

"Than . . . to be inducted into the Army."

But David Schine had gone into the Army, a very special private who received very special privileges and attention. For example, Secretary Stevens had McCarthy and Cohn flown to Fort Dix in his own army plane so that they could visit with

Schine, and then they were flown on to Boston where McCarthy had attacked the Army for being soft on Communism.

"I had been cooperating right along with the Senator and his committee. . . ." Stevens protested, bewildered by what was happening to him, to his authority, to his position as civilian chief of the army. "And I want it to continue. Mr. Cohn indicated that Senator McCarthy was very mad and felt that I had double-crossed him."

But Stevens had not been able to appease the appetite of the Senator or to fight him successfully. McCarthy had insisted in a letter to the Secretary that "Mr. Schine would never have been drafted except because of the fact that he worked for my committee."

When it came his turn to question Stevens, McCarthy was anxious to shatter the credibility of the Army case. "Now," he demanded aggressively, "can you tell us today whether or not you wanted the hearings at Fort Monmouth suspended?"

(The workers at Monmouth, civilian and military, had been laboring, among other matters, on systems designed to give early warning of a possible enemy missile attack. Any disruption of that work could slow the entire defense effort, perhaps leave the country insufficiently guarded. Actually, McCarthy and his people had done far less investigating than "suggesting" various employees might be security risks.)

Stevens responded: "I wanted them suspended in order that the Army could carry out the hearings themselves and stop the panic that was being created in the minds of the public on a basis that was not justified by the facts."

McCarthy ignored the substance of the answer. "How did you finally succeed in getting the hearings suspended?" he asked.

"How did I succeed?"

"Yes; they are suspended as of today. How did you succeed?"

"They aren't suspended as far as I know."

"Bob, don't give me that. You know that the hearings were suspended the day you or someone else filed your charges against Mr. Cohn, Mr. Carr and myself. . . ."

For fourteen days, the Secretary of the Army sat in the witness chair, questioned incessantly by Senator McCarthy. Stevens' energy and strength ebbed steadily, even as the Senator repeated himself or his questions became increasingly less pertinent to the matters at issue. At times tears appeared in Stevens' eyes, and he seemed incapable of going on under the repeated hammering of McCarthy and then Ray Jenkins. At one point, Joseph Welch broke in, mild of manner but no less firm for being so.

"I am informed, Mr. Jenkins, that you have tried many murder trials, and with great success. But may I remind you, my friend, that this is not a murder trial and that you are examining the Secretary of the Army."

Yet when Chairman Mundt announced that Stevens could be excused at his own request, Welch objected. "Mr. Stevens . . . would not permit me to ask for quarter. He would prefer to go on rather than see any signal flag go up of any lack of courage on his part."

Commented Senator McCarthy, "I have no personal sympathy for this particular witness."

And so McCarthy tried to display Secretary Stevens as a man who wanted to coddle Communists, who catered to the personal wishes of an ordinary private soldier, who seemed unable to make a fight or win it, a man opposed to the procedures of the Senate.

It was McCarthy, in fact, who stood against the established order of doing things. He was committed to acting out his private vision of right and wrong regardless of the law or custom or who might suffer as a result. Nowhere was this demonstrated more than when a confidential letter from J. Edgar Hoover to the intelligence branch of the Army came under discussion. The letter had been stolen by a government worker and passed on to McCarthy.

Senator McClellan crystallized the issue of the letter as "whether a Senate subcommittee is entitled to gain by theft what it cannot legally obtain by subpoena."

McCarthy's response was to accuse McClellan of trying to railroad him into jail. But the Arkansas Senator, though not one of McCarthy's fervent supporters, was a much less dangerous adversary than the lawyer from Boston.

Attorney Welch was curious about the circumstances surrounding the so-called FBI letter. "Senator McCarthy, when you took the stand, you knew of course that you were going to be asked about the letter, did you not?"

"I assumed that would be the subject."

"And you of course understood that you were going to be asked the source from which you got it?"

"I won't answer that."

Welch was undismayed. "Could I have the oath you took read to us wholly by the reporter?"

Chairman Mundt extracted the pipe from his mouth. "Mr. Welch, that doesn't seem to be an appropriate question. . . . It's the same oath you took."

Welch was aware of that. "The oath included a promise," he reminded Senator McCarthy, "a solemn promise by you to tell the truth and nothing but the truth. Is that correct, sir?"

McCarthy shook his head from side to side. "Mr. Welch, you are not the first individual that tried to get me to betray the confidence and give out the names of my informants. You will be no more successful than those who have tried it in the past."

"I am only asking you, sir, did you realize when you took the oath that you were making a solemn promise to tell the truth to this committee?"

"I understand the oath, Mr. Welch."

"And when you took it, did you have some mental reservation, some Fifth or Sixth Amendment notion that you could measure what you would tell?"

"I don't take the Fifth Amendment."

"Have you some private reservation when you take the oath that . . . lets you be the judge of what you will testify to?"

The New England lawyer had opened wide the jaws of his trap, a trap baited with the Senator's own past words and actions. McCarthy was able to find no way of avoiding it.

"The answer is that there is no reservation about telling the whole truth."

"Thank you, sir. Then tell us who delivered the document to you?"

"You will not get the information."

"You wish then to put your own interpretation on your oath and tell us less than the whole truth?"

"You can go right ahead and try until doomsday. You will not get the names of any informants who rely upon me to protect them."

"Will you tell us where you were when you got it?"

"No."

"Were you in Washington?"

"The answer was I would not tell you."

"How soon after you got it did you show it to anyone?"

"I don't remember."

"To whom did you first show it?"

"I don't recall."

So it went. From McCarthy refusals, evasions, questionable failures of memory. McCarthy, the investigator, so quick to challenge the right of citizens to invoke their constitutional privilege, refused to abide by his sworn oath to tell the truth. Here was McCarthy setting himself up as a special case, beyond the law, beyond the systems by which the society functioned, exhibiting no respect for anyone or anything other than his own desires— all under the red eyes of the television cameras, in full view of twenty million Americans.

Among McCarthy's countercharges was this: "Five days after the Secretary claimed that attempts were made to induce and persuade him by improper means to give preferential treatment to Private Schine, Mr. Stevens posed for smiling photographs with Private Schine at Fort Dix."

Roy Cohn had told Counsel Jenkins that he had "proof" of "bad faith" on the part of the Army, and Jenkins accepted his word as fact.

With Cohn in the witness chair, Jenkins began his questioning. "You stated to me . . . that Mr. Stevens as Secretary of the Army on that date [November 12, 1953] requested David Schine to be photographed with him?"

"I stated that," Cohn said. "And that is the fact, sir. . . . I told you, sir, I believe, that I thought very substantial proof of the bad faith of Mr. Stevens in making these charges now was the fact that, long after the threats had supposedly been made, . . . Mr. Stevens was not only solicitous of Private Schine but . . . asked that he be photographed with Private Schine. . . ."

"I will ask you whether or not you told me that you had documentary evidence in the form of a photograph of Mr. Stevens and Mr. Schine corroborating your statement to me that Mr. Stevens requested his photograph be taken with Schine. Is that correct?"

"I told you, sir, that as far as I knew there was a picture of Mr. Stevens and Private Schine taken on November seventeenth. . . ."

"Did you or not tell me it was taken on that occasion at the request of the Secretary of the Army?"

"I said that then," Cohn replied, "and I say that now."

Secretary Stevens was to testify to the contrary. Jenkins asked him, "Did you ever at your suggestion at a meeting anywhere, any time, say that 'I want my picture taken with David' and have it done?"

"I'm sure I never made a statement just like you make it there," was Stevens's answer.

At that Ray Jenkins brought out an enlargement of a photograph showing the Secretary with David Schine in uniform. Stevens was flustered, and Jenkins moved in. "Isn't it a fact that you were being especially nice and considerate and tender of this boy Schine—" Stevens tried to interrupt but Jenkins pressed on. "Wait! Wait! Wait! Wait!—in order to dissuade the Senator from continuing his investigation of one of your departments?"

"Positively and completely not!"

It seemed, however, as if McCarthy and Cohn had scored a major triumph, and they had that night in which to gloat. But only that night. The next morning, Joseph Welch turned a new and penetrating light on the issue of the photograph. He addressed the entire subcommittee.

"Mr. Chairman, Mr. Jenkins yesterday was imposed upon as was the Secretary of the Army by having a doctored or altered photograph produced in this courtroom as if it were honest." He brought forth a photograph. "I show you now a photograph, in respect of which I charge that what was offered in evidence yesterday was an altered, shamefully cut-down picture, so that somebody could say to Stevens, 'Were you not photographed alone with David Schine,' when the truth is he was photographed in a group."

The group in the picture presented by Mr. Welch showed Stevens, Schine and Francis Carr, along with army Colonel Jack Bradley, a man Schine claimed as a close friend.

An uproar broke out in the Caucus Room. McCarthy interrupted, disputing what Welch had said, demanding the lawyer be put under oath. Senator Symington insisted that McCarthy was out of order.

"Oh, be quiet!" McCarthy rumbled in return. "I am getting awfully sick of sitting down here at the end of the table and having whomever wants to interrupt in the middle of a sentence. . . . I suggest the chair make the record clear that Mr. Welch was not speaking the truth. . . ."

Gradually the furor subsided, and Ray Jenkins started to question Roy Cohn again, anxious to clear the air. "Was anything ever said to me up to this time about any person being cut out of that photograph?"

"No, sir. I do not think anything was said. . . ."

Cohn went on to say he had seen a picture of Schine and Stevens in Schine's office but couldn't remember if there was anyone else in it.

Emphasizing the importance of the photograph was the memory of the major role a doctored picture had played in defeating Millard Tydings for reelection in Maryland. And of course McCarthy and Cohn had made this recent picture part of their charges against the Army. Despite this, Cohn was able years later to write off this moment: "Joe Welch, with his sense of drama and excellent timing, managed to create a major event out of an essentially trivial incident and thus divert people's attention from the central issue." But to many people at the time of the hearing, the central issue was the questionable techniques and the insincerity of Senator McCarthy and his aides in pursuit of their own ends, a fact Cohn and his superior seemed unable to grasp.

James Juliana, a member of McCarthy's staff, was called to testify. Joseph Welch asked him why the "whole" picture that Roy Cohn remembered seeing on David Schine's wall had not been produced.

"I wasn't asked for it," Juliana answered.

"You were asked for something different from the thing that hung on Schine's wall?"

"I never knew what hung on Schine's wall. . . ."

In his soft voice, Welch persisted: "Did you think this came from a pixie? Where did you think this picture that I hold in my hand came from?"

"I had no idea."

Senator McCarthy chose this moment to interrupt. It was a mistake, the kind of mistake he never fully understood, or seemed able to avoid. "Will the counsel for my benefit define—I think he might be an expert on that—what a pixie is?"

Welch was pleased to oblige: "Yes. I should say, Mr. Senator, that a pixie is a close relative of a fairy. Shall I proceed, sir? Have I enlightened you?"

The Caucus Room erupted with laughter. The laughter was with Joseph Welch, at Joe McCarthy.

Roy Cohn, too, had been making mistakes during his testimony. Secure in his swift rise to national prominence, in the strength of his flexible intelligence, of his growing importance, he was by his own subsequent description "rambling, garrulous, repetitious. I was brash, smug, and smart-alecky. I was pompous and petulant." No one would argue with that self-description.

Roy Cohn, he announced for all to hear, "is here speaking for Roy Cohn, to give the facts."

He grandly informed the Senators that he would be "glad to answer any question that any member of the committee wants to ask."

He sought to direct Attorney Jenkins: "I wonder if we could do it this way. . . ."

He tried vainly to match wits with Joseph Welch. When Cohn indicated that he did not have a legal counsel, Welch said, "Mr.

Cohn, I assume you would like it understood that, although I sit at the same table, I am not your counsel."

Cohn grinned smugly. "There is not a statement that has been made at this hearing with which I am in more complete agreement."

"In all modesty, sir," Welch returned. "I am content that it should appear from my end that I am not your counsel."

This time the onlookers laughed at Roy Cohn. It was a warning he and Senator McCarthy might have heeded. Public men laughed at are seldom taken seriously.

XV

A STOLEN LETTER, A PRIVATE MEETING, A FORGETFUL SECRETARY

THE HEARINGS CONTINUED, WITH A CHANGING CAST OF CHARacters, each playing out his own role. Lies were given and laid to rest, chicanery and solid principle were made evident, private interest was revealed as was public concern, the weaknesses of Senators were exposed, and pettiness alongside generosity of spirit. And always there was Senator McCarthy, head hanging down, face closed, eyes hooded, the muffled voice harsh and monotonous, interrupting, attacking, demanding time for his incessant points of order, uttering disjointed monologues that ranged far afield. And the television cameras showed it all to a world increasingly concerned by what it was seeing.

Counselor to the Department of the Army John Adams testified to the abuse he had taken from Roy Cohn and of his complaints about this to Senator McCarthy. "He [Cohn] said," Adams recalled, "that he would teach me what it meant to go over his head. I said to him, 'Roy, is that a threat?' He said, 'No, that's a promise.' . . . I could talk only to him."

Adams described telephone calls from Cohn that were abusive, often obscene. And another witness, a Colonel BeLieu, described Cohn's language as being "a little lower than a mule skinner's."

When Adams had suggested that there was a strong possibility that David Schine might be sent overseas, Cohn had made what was perhaps his most damaging statement. "We'll wreck the Army!" Adams reported him as having said angrily.

Roy Cohn was on vacation at the Boca Raton Hotel and Club in Florida (G. David Schine, president and general manager) when he learned on January 18, 1954, of the Army's plans for Private Schine. The next day, John Adams informed the Special Committee, he had received a call from Francis Carr summoning "certain members of the Army Loyalty and Security Appeal Board for questioning. . . ." Adams had objected to this clear threat to the Army's authority.

"This was a matter of vital importance to the Army," he explained under oath. "The boards are quasi-judicial in nature. . . . The Army always felt that to subject their actions to review by other bodies would be similar to requiring a judge to appear before a legislature to explain the reasons for his decision.

"We knew that the performance of these difficult tasks would be jeopardized, and objectivity would be lost. . . ."

Concerned about what was happening, Adams had looked for advice. With Secretary Stevens then in the Pacific area on official business, he went to H. Struve Hensel, general counsel of the Defense Department. Hensel passed him on to Deputy Attorney General William Rogers. On January 21, Rogers arranged a meeting of dramatic importance. Present in the office of Attorney General Herbert Brownell, in addition to Rogers, were Sherman Adams, Presidential Assistant, and Senator Henry Cabot Lodge, Jr., of Massachusetts. After listening to Adams' story of his dealings with McCarthy and his aides, in support of Adams' position, Sherman Adams told him to take the precaution of writing down everything that had happened. Also, he suggested that John Adams report his experience to the other Senators serving on the McCarthy Committee. Both suggestions were followed, and as a result, the subpoenas for loyalty board members were canceled.

In the opinion of President Eisenhower, the public airing of this series of events—the January 21 meeting, the activities of the Army Security Board, etc.—was to the detriment of the national good, and he now acted to counter the trend, to eliminate legislative interference in the Executive Branch. A letter was sent from the White House to Secretary of Defense Charles Wilson banning any further testimony on the January 21 meeting or any other exchanges *within* the Executive Branch.

This letter must have rocked McCarthy, since his self-appointed status as protector of the national good was being questioned at the top. At the same time, he was being reminded of the constitutional separation of powers, of the division between the executive and legislative branches of the government. He was being bluntly told that certain areas were officially off-limits to him, were none of his business. For the first time, the enormous power and influence of the Executive Branch were aligned against him.

Equally intimidating was the immense popular prestige of President Eisenhower. The letter recalled what Eisenhower had said in his first message to Congress: "Primary responsibility for keeping out the disloyal and the dangerous rests squarely upon the Executive Branch. When this branch so conducts itself as to require policing by another branch of the Government, it invites its own disorder and confusion."

In practice, however, the separation of powers *was* being violated. Loyalty board reports were being turned over to Senator McCarthy covertly. These were often incomplete or unevaluated, made while investigations were still in progress. And the issuance of the subpoenas to members of the loyalty boards was clearly a raw effort to bring them under McCarthy's control, a thrust for illegitimate power that neither the Army nor the President dared ignore.

There was also the FBI "letter" illegally delivered to McCarthy. Continuation of such disregard for proper orderly procedure could bring about a breakdown in the government structure.

The President recognized the investigatory obligations of the legislature and intended to make sure that information within the jurisdiction of such committees was supplied them, but he insisted in his letter to Defense Secretary Charles Wilson that the ultimate "responsibility for the conduct of the Executive Branch rests with the President."

He made clear also that Presidents have traditionally censored the release of information when not to do so would conflict with the public welfare or endanger national security. The letter went on: "Because it is essential to efficient and effective administration that employees of the Executive Branch be in a position to be completely candid in advising with each other on official matters, and because it is not in the public interest that any of their conversations or communications be disclosed, you will instruct employees of your Department that, in all of their appearances before the Subcommittee of the Senate Committee on Government Operations regarding the inquiry now before it, they are not to testify to communications or to produce any such documents or reproductions. This principle must be maintained regardless of who would be benefited by such disclosures."

McCarthy's initial response to the President's action was uncharacteristic. "I must admit," he muttered, "that I am somewhat at a loss as to know what to do. . . ." He recovered quickly, denouncing the "iron curtain" that had been drawn over the January 21 meeting, saying of the President that "if he knew what this was all about, he would not sign an order that you cannot tell a Senate committee what went on when they cooked up those charges against Mr. Cohn, Mr. Carr and myself."

It was a crisis for the Senator, and he needed time to decide how to deal with it. This resulted in a recess of one week. When the hearings reconvened, Roy Cohn tried to prove that the McCarthy Committee's concern with the Army had begun four months before the Army's concern with Private Schine. To support this contention, he produced a memorandum by Paul Crouch, a professional informer then being investigated by the Department of Justice for perjury. Crouch had been an employee of the McCarthy Committee, though the Democratic members of the committee had not known of his employment.

Senator McClellan asked for an explanation. He was a member of the subcommittee, McClellan said, but he had never before heard of the Crouch memorandum. Why? McCarthy's response was fired with patriotic fervor: "I would like to make it clear that I think that the oath which every person in government takes to protect and defend this country against all enemies . . . that oath towers far above any Presidential secrecy directive. . . ."

Thinking about the purloined FBI "letter," McClellan said, "You may be right, but I do not know of any oath that any man ever took that required him to commit a crime."

McCarthy ignored the remark. He had decided to do battle with President Eisenhower and proceeded to challenge Presidential authority. "I would like to notify two million Federal employees," he droned insistently, "that I feel that it is their duty to give us any information which they have about graft, corruption, Communists and treason, and that there is no loyalty to a superior officer which can tower above and beyond their loyalty to their country."

Again it was Senator McClellan who sliced through McCarthy's cloudy rhetoric to the core of the question: "If this principle is adopted—that every Federal employee shall reveal everything he knows—then you have no security system in America. It will be destroyed totally and irrevocably if all who have information give it out indiscriminately."

Chairman Mundt, anxious to end the debate, termed the discussion "irrelevant," apparently unable to recognize the profound Constitutional question involved. But the White House, sensitive to the problem, responded to McCarthy's remarks:

> The obligation and duties of the executive, judicial, and legislative branches of the government are defined by the Constitution. The Executive Branch . . . has the sole and fundamental responsibility under the Constitution for the enforcement of our laws and presidential orders.
>
> That responsibility cannot be usurped by any individual who may seek to set himself above the laws of our land or to override the orders of the President of the United States to Federal employees of the Executive . . .

McCarthy then uttered an amazing remark for an elected representative by stating that Federal officials were "bound only by their oath."

"Then," replied Senator McClellan, "you are advocating government by the individual conscience as against government by law?"

"No phony stamp of secrecy should keep from the Congress any evidence of wrongdoing."

"Then no committee member is under any obligation to protect the wrongdoer," McClellan replied logically.

McCarthy ignored logic when it suited him. It suited him now. "I have instructed a vast number of Federal employees that they are duty-bound to give me information even though some little bureaucrat has stamped it 'secret' to defend himself."

McClellan fired back. "I am sorry to hear you refer to Mr. J. Edgar Hoover as 'some little bureaucrat'."

"Senator, I will just not abide by any secrecy directive. You and I have seen and will see Presidents come and go."

"Senators, too."

"The issue is whether the people are entitled to the facts."

"No," McClellan replied. "The issue is whether a Senate subcommittee is entitled to gain by theft what it cannot legally obtain by subpoena."

The issue was crystal clear. It had gone far beyond McCarthy, Cohn or even the Department of the Army. This was a fight between those who defended the Constitution and those who chose to attack or to disregard its provisions, whatever their stated reasons. The question being asked was whether the United States was a government run by law or by the whim of men. The battle continued.

On the first day of June, eleven documents were introduced in purported support of Senator McCarthy's claims that the Army, in the persons of Secretary Stevens and John Adams, had used bribery and blackmail to get the McCarthy Committee to end its investigation. The eleven memoranda were signed by either McCarthy, Roy Cohn or Francis Carr. Copies of the documents were distributed to the press even before McCarthy's fellow Republicans on the committee knew of their existence.

In the story he wrote for the Chicago *Sun-Times,* Carleton Kent commented on the way Senator McCarthy guarded the documents, and he mentioned their newness.

The Army's reaction to the documents was that they were false.

The next day Roy Cohn testified under oath that all the memoranda had been dictated to McCarthy's personal secretary, Mrs.

Mary Brinkley Driscoll. A grandmother, Mrs. Driscoll had run McCarthy's office for six years. When called upon to testify, she displayed a great deal of nervousness, and Ray Jenkins questioned her gently. "Do you recall the dictation of the memos?"

Mrs. Driscoll shook her head. "I couldn't," she said in a low voice. "I have too much dictation."

Her shorthand notebooks—had she kept them? "I never keep shorthand notebooks."

Jenkins indicated the old frayed file from which the new memoranda had been extracted. "Were the copies made after the Army release?"

"I think so."

"That particular file now is just identified by the words 'Investigating Committee'."

"That is right."

"Is that all?"

"That is all it says."

"How did you know where to go to look for the file, Mrs. Driscoll?"

"I can't tell you that, Mr. Jenkins."

During this questioning, Roy Cohn sat close by offering whispered advice, and Senator McCarthy passed notes along to Mrs. Driscoll.

None of this satisfied Ray Jenkins and he was becoming concerned. Mrs. Driscoll was his witness, called to substantiate the authenticity of the eleven documents. He was determined to have her do so. "I ask you," he said, "to examine the memoranda to see if you typed them as originals."

"I think," she answered, "they may be the originals as typed by me but I can't tell you positively."

An anticipatory stillness filled the Caucus Room as Joseph Welch prepared to question Mrs. Driscoll. Assessing her as a tense and frightened woman, he faced his task with no particular relish. Elbow leaning on the long table, his spectacles held high in a characteristic pose, he began:

"When did you start working on the file?"

She hesitated. "I don't have any recollection."

Welch knew that the memoranda had been typed on three different machines; he was equally certain that Mrs. Driscoll was aware of this. He asked on which machine the first memorandum had been typed.

"I couldn't tell you," she replied in a thin voice. "I don't know."

"You don't know!"

"I don't recognize the typing. . . ."

"The one at your desk is an IBM. Is that right?"

"There is an IBM at my desk now."

"Was it there then?"

"I don't recall. I don't know."

"Don't you know when you got it?"

"No."

It was impossible for Welch to let that pass. "You can't tell us whether you've had it a month or two or longer?"

"No, Mr. Welch, I can't."

"You have no memory at all?"

"No. A typewriter is a typewriter, and I don't pay any attention to the type of typewriter."

Welch was compelled to challenge that: "You are a paragon of virtue! My secretaries are always kicking about them and wanting a new one. You don't pay any attention to them?"

Mrs. Driscoll seemed thoroughly flustered, and Senator McCarthy attempted to help her. He claimed he was unable to understand what Welch was driving at, found his questions absurd and irrelevant.

The Boston lawyer raised his brows but not his voice. "I'm interested to know whether these memoranda are the real McCoy or not! You know that, don't you!"

Abruptly McCarthy seemed to lose interest. He had other problems. That same afternoon, Senator Ralph Flanders had made a blistering attack against him on the floor of the Senate.

Welch, however, was still concerned with Mrs. Driscoll. He drew from her testimony that she had placed the eleven memoranda in a file that no one else was able to locate. Then he proceeded to read to her a memorandum presumably written by Francis Carr on March 10, the same day that McCarthy first learned of the Army report on David Schine:

" 'Senator McCarthy advised Mr. Seaton [Assistant Secretary of Defense] that the writer was searching the files for memoranda dictated concerning Schine'."

Welch turned back to Mrs. Driscoll. "Were you startled when Carr dictated that to you?"

"No."

"Did you say to him, 'Mr. Carr, look no further, I've got 'em all here in the slickest little package you ever saw'?"

"Absolutely not!"

"Did you tell him his search was silly?"

"Of course I didn't!"

Welch made his point unmistakable. "Well, you had them all together, didn't you?"

Her answer, when it came, was weak and unconvincing. "Maybe I overlooked one."

When he subsequently summed up Mrs. Driscoll's appearance, Welch concluded that her credibility was open to question, her testimony "an amazing structure, was built, not brick by brick, but all at once, when a shelter was badly needed."

XVI

NO SENSE OF DECENCY

PEOPLE EVERYWHERE WERE CONCENTRATED ON MCCARTHY, Cohn, Welch, Jenkins, Schine, Stevens, the Senators and the staff of the Special Committee. The hearings were the overwhelming attraction on television and drew more attention, critical and popular, than *I Love Lucy* or Ed Sullivan. Newspapers each day were crowded with the details, with comments on the characters of the players and their diverse styles.

Ray Jenkins, plain-spoken, strong, was readily cast as an honest and implacable law officer. Joseph Welch, quizzical, quiet, nevertheless was shrewd and relentless in achieving his ends. Karl Mundt, with his ever-present pipe, seemed somehow not quite in control as chairman. Joe McCarthy was aggressively confident, certain of his power and his following, attacking, able to turn each simple question into a snide suggestion of improper behavior. And Roy Cohn was darkly wary, quick, arrogant.

Up to now it had been reasonable to assume that Senator

McCarthy commanded widespread support among the officers and men of the armed forces. They, after all, were in the front line against any aggressor, and McCarthy had claimed the battleground against Communism as his own. But it was becoming dramatically evident that this fight was more likely to undercut the cause of freedom. In dragging the Army through a tumultuous and acrimonious dispute over an army private of no distinction, McCarthy was denigrating the service to which those men were dedicated.

For Joe McCarthy method and motive were inextricably entwined, and he showed no sign of changing. Late in the afternoon of the thirtieth day of the hearings, he came at last to the witness chair at the great coffin-shaped table in the Caucus Room. To one side of him was Roy Cohn, Francis Carr to the other. For the Senator's use, a large colored map had been set up.

It was Ray Jenkins's hope in questioning McCarthy to lead him along a path that would display the Senator as a hardworking patriot, informed, reasonable, efficient—in short, a man sincerely doing a job that needed doing. "Your position on Communism," Jenkins asked, "is well known, Senator?"

McCarthy replied happily, "I think so."

"Your viewpoint, you would say, and their viewpoint [the Communists'] are diametrically opposed to each other?"

"That is right."

"You are not one of their fair-haired boys?"

"You are right."

"You have never been tendered their nomination by the Communist Party for the Presidency—is that what you mean?"

"Not yet."

Jenkins then asked McCarthy to inform America what "the set-up of the Communists is."

The Senator went to his map. He pointed out the names and addresses of Communist leaders around the country. But even at this late moment there was little meat on the bones of his presentation. Some of the names he offered were of people already dead; one was of a totally patriotic American in a southern state; others were of people who had long ago severed their connections with Communism. There were no subversives. No spies. No security risks.

The most damaging thrust of McCarthy's presentation—in fact, his entire approach to the menace of Communism—lay in an attitude which stated implicitly that by attacking clerks and librarians overseas and army officers domestically, by questioning the motives of elected or appointed officials, by applying the tarbrush of "treason" to loyal Americans, by unloosing gross and unsubstantiated charges against any one who opposed his policies, the tide of Communist aggression would somehow be turned back.

For those who chose not to weigh and sift through its beclouding rhetoric, McCarthyism appeared to be the answer to the nation's troubles. For too many persons it had become comforting to blame all difficulties, native and alien, on an internal conspiracy, and having located such a conspiracy, at least in one's mind, it was easy also to find a simple solution to all problems: Make the conspirators go away, and the problems would disappear with them.

Reality, however, failed to support this contention. None of this would end the rising inflation or the injustices done the black people of America. Neither would it end the troubles in Indochina or Tibet or Berlin. It could not wipe out starvation in India or eliminate the slums of Italy, or the blight of purse and spirit in Portugal and Spain. It would not solve the racial conflict in South Africa or eliminate the differences between Israelis and Arabs in the Middle East. Nor would it put an end to the imperialist designs of the Soviet Union or the belligerency of Communist China.

"There are people," McCarthy said as he continued to testify, "who think that we can live side by side with Communists." He rejected that prospect out of hand. "There is not the remotest possibility of this war which we are in today, and it is a war . . . ending except by victory or by death for this civilization." This was another easy answer, ignoring the complexities of the struggle for peace by accepting the inevitability of war and total destruction.

How to prevent the catastrophe? McCarthy had an answer for that. The people would have to "depend upon those of us whom they send down here to man the watchtowers of the nation. . . ." In other words, in a Federal structure formed of checks and balances, which had been created to spread and dilute power and authority and to lodge final control in the hands of an informed electorate, McCarthy insisted that men like himself should be the last arbiters of loyalty and patriotism. No room existed in his argument for legitimate difference of opinion, for searching debate. He was the one who should assume the power of the Executive Branch and dig out those who failed to agree with him.

It was a typical McCarthy performance, but it was too little and came too late. Though he seemed oblivious to it, the end for Joseph Raymond McCarthy had come earlier that same day.

Roy Cohn did him in.

Roy Cohn and David Schine. And Joe McCarthy's inability to behave within the limits established by civilized men so they may live with each other in relative tranquillity.

Roy Cohn was again in the witness chair that morning, hoping to present the McCarthy Committee's side of the controversy. Behind him was his first experience as a witness, and he was certain that he had profited from it. He was determined to correct past errors, to display a more affirmative face to the millions of people watching. He intended to be, he wrote later, "unruffled . . . deferential . . . withdrawn . . . would speak to the point." Tucked out of sight was the arrogance, the bright young man on the make, the smart-aleckness; the hard edge of the aggressive young lawyer was softened. A completely different Roy Cohn was on display.

Ray Jenkins guided the new Cohn through a series of questions designed to reveal Cohn's skill as a hunter of Communists, his expertise about espionage, his cunning about subversive activity. Jenkins also established that Mr. Cohn and Mr. Schine were good friends, and there was nothing wrong with that. Finished at last, he turned Cohn over to Joseph Welch for questioning.

Mr. Welch addressed himself to the situation at Fort Monmouth. He brought out that in March or April Roy Cohn "knew about the situation of possible subversives and security risks, and even spies at Fort Monmouth, is that right?"

"Yes, sir," Cohn replied.

"And I think," Welch went on, "you have used the word 'disturbing'—that you found it a disturbing situation?"

"Yes, sir."

"And you had, so to speak, only a sort of glimpse in it, you couldn't tell how big it was or how little it was, could you?"

"Not at the beginning, sir."

"And you probably knew enough about Fort Monmouth or found out quickly enough about Fort Monmouth, to know that it was a sensitive place, didn't you?"

"Yes, sir."

"And I am sure the knowledge that you had was a source, Mr. Cohn, to one in your position, of some anxiety for the nation's safety wasn't it?"

"It was one situation among a number of serious situations, yes, sir."

Welch displayed his sympathy. "Well, I don't know how

many worries you have, but I am sure that was, to you, a disturbing and alarming situation."

"Well, sir," Cohn answered, "it was certainly serious enough for me to want to check into it and see how many facts we could check out and—"

"And stop it as soon as possible?" Welch prompted.

"Well, it was a question of developing the—"

Attorney Welch persisted: "But the thing that we have to do is stop it, isn't it?"

"Stop what, sir?"

"Stop the risk."

"Stop the risk, sir?"

"Yes."

"Yes," Cohn agreed at last, "what we had to do was stop the risk and—"

"That is right," Welch said cheerfully, "get the people suspended or get them on trial or fire them or do something. That is right, isn't it?"

"Partly, sir."

"But it is primarily the thing, isn't it?"

"Well, the thing came up—"

Welch focused on the young man across the long, dark, shining table. "Mr. Cohn, if I told you now that we had a bad situation at Monmouth, you would want to cure it by sundown, if you could, wouldn't you?"

Cohn, a trained lawyer, thought he could perceive Welch's intentions. He answered carefully, "I am sure I couldn't, sir."

"But you would like to, if you could?"

"No, what I want—"

"Answer me," Welch demanded. "That must be right. It has to be right."

"What I would like to do and what can be done are two different things."

"Well, if you could be God and do anything you wish, you would cure it by sundown, wouldn't you?"

Cohn conceded that he would do precisely that.

"And you were that alarmed about Monmouth?" Welch said.

"It doesn't go that way."

"I am just asking how it does go. When you find there are Communists and possible spies in a place like Monmouth, you must be alarmed, aren't you?"

"Now you have asked me how it goes, and I'm going to tell you."

"No, I didn't ask you how it goes. I said aren't you alarmed when you find it is there?"

Cohn wanted to support the past actions of the McCarthy Committee and his own behavior. "Whenever I hear that people have been failing to act on FBI information about Communists, I do think it is alarming. I would like the Communists out, and I would like to be able to advise this committee of why people who have the responsibility for getting them out haven't carried out their responsibility."

Joe McCarthy himself could not have put it better. But Joseph Welch was not deterred. "Yes," he agreed, "but what you want first of all, Mr. Cohn—and let's be fair with each other—what you want first of all, if it is within your power, is to get them out, isn't it?"

"I don't know if I'd draw a distinction as to what ought to come first, Mr. Welch."

"It certainly ranks terrifically high, doesn't it?" Welch asked.

"It was a situation that I thought should be developed, and we did develop it."

"When did you first meet Secretary Stevens?"

Cohn was specific: "I first met Secretary Stevens September seventh, I believe it was."

"And you knew that he was the new Secretary of the Army?"

"Yes, I did know he was the Secretary of the Army."
"And you must have had high hopes about him, didn't you?"
"I don't think I gave it too much thought, sir."
Welch would not let that pass. "Anybody wants the Secretary of the Army to do well, no matter what party he is from, do we not?"
Cohn had to agree. "Surely, sir."
"And on September seventh, when you met him, you had in your bosom this alarming situation about Monmouth, is that right?"
"Yes, I knew about Monmouth then. Yes, sir."
"And you didn't tug at his lapel and say, Mr. Secretary, I know something about Monmouth that won't let me sleep nights? You didn't do it, did you?"

Watching and listening, Senator McCarthy was at first amused by the dialogue between Cohn and Welch, but soon he became more and more unsettled. He glowered from under heavy brows at the New England lawyer, ran his tongue around the inside of his mouth, his anger mounting by visible degrees. His eyes seemed to withdraw, and his face with its perpetual shadow-beard grew darker, more ominous.

Roy Cohn tried to respond to the question. "I don't—as I testified, Mr. Welch—I don't know whether I talked to Mr. Stevens about it then or not. I know that on the sixteenth I did. Whether I talked to him on the seventh or not is something I don't know."

The answer failed to satisfy Welch. "Don't you know that, if you had really told him what your fears were, and substantiated them to any extent, he could have jumped in the next day with suspensions?"
"No, sir."
"Did you then have any reason to doubt his fidelity?"
"No, sir."
"Or his honor?"

"No."

"Or his patriotism?"

"No."

"And yet, Mr. Cohn, you didn't tell him what you knew?"

"I don't know whether I did or not. I told him some of the things I knew, sir. I don't think I told him everything I knew on the first occasion. After the first two or three sessions, I think he had a pretty good idea of what we were working on."

"Mr. Cohn," Welch said, "tell me once more: Every time you learn of a Communist, of a spy anywhere, is it your policy to get them out as fast as possible?"

"Surely, we want them out as fast as possible, sir."

"And whenever you learn of one from now on, Mr. Cohn, I beg of you, will you tell somebody about them quick."

"Mr. Welch, with great respect, I work for the committee here. They know how we go about handling situations of Communist infiltration. If they are displeased with the speed with which I and the group of men who work with me proceed, if they are displeased with the order in which we move, I am sure they will give me appropriate instructions along those lines, and I will follow any which they give me."

A small smile turned the corners of Joseph Welch's mouth. "May I add my small voice, sir, and say whenever you know about a subversive or a Communist or a spy, please hurry. Will you remember those words?"

Joe McCarthy could remain silent no more. Words rumbled out from between lips that barely moved. "Mr. Chairman, in view of that question . . ."

"Have you a point of order?" Senator Mundt asked.

At that moment, typically, McCarthy struck out in the only way he knew—he attacked. Blindly, with the nearest weapon at hand. Equally typical, the effect he had on those watching and listening was lost to him.

"Mr. Chairman," he droned, "in view of Mr. Welch's request

that the information be given once we know of anyone who might be performing any work for the Communist Party, I think we should tell him that he has in his law firm a young man—whom he recommended, incidentally, to do work on this committee—who has been for a number of years a member of an organization which was named, oh, years and years ago, as the legal bulwark of the Communist Party, an organization which always swings to the defense of anyone who dares to expose Communists. I certainly assume that Mr. Welch did not know of this young man at the time he recommended him as the assistant counsel for this committee. But he has such terror and such a great desire to know where anyone is located who may be serving the Communist cause, Mr. Welch, that I thought we should just call to your attention the fact that your Mr. Fisher—who is still in your law firm today, whom you asked to have down here looking over the secret and classified material—is a member of an organization, not named by me but named by various committees—named by the Attorney General, as I recall, and I think I quote this verbatim—as the legal bulwark of the Communist Party. He belonged to that for a sizable number of years, according to his own admission, and he belonged to it long after it had been exposed as the legal arm of the Communist Party."

An anticipatory hush descended over the Caucus Room as the McCarthy monologue ran on. In the witness chair, Roy Cohn paled suddenly, appeared startled by what his chief was doing.

McCarthy, oblivious to all reactions, rumbled ahead. "Knowing that, Mr. Welch, I just felt that I had a duty to respond to your urgent request that before sundown, when we know of anyone serving the Communist cause, we let the agency know. We are now letting you know that your man did belong to this organization for either three or four years, belonged to it long after he was out of law school.

"I don't think you can find any place, anywhere, an organization which had done more to defend Communists—I am again quoting the report—to defend Communists, to defend espionage agents and to aid the Communist cause, than the man whom you originally wanted down here at your right hand instead of Mr. St. Clair.

"I have hesitated bringing that up, but I have been rather bored with your phony request to Mr. Cohn here that he personally get every Communist out of government before sundown. Therefore, we will give you information about the young man in your own organization.

"I am not asking you at this time to explain why you tried to foist him on this committee. Whether you knew he was a member of that Communist organization or not, I don't know. I assume you did not, Mr. Welch, because I get the impression that, while you're quite an actor, you play for a laugh, I don't think you have any conception of the danger of the Communist Party. I don't think you yourself would ever knowingly aid the Communist cause. I think you are unknowingly aiding it when you try to burlesque this hearing in which we are attempting to bring out the facts, however."

Welch, face drained of blood, eyes gone moist, stared at McCarthy with disbelief and horror etched in every line of his face. "Senator McCarthy," he started out, "I did not know—"

Senator Mundt broke in. "Mr. Welch," he said, "the chair should say he has no recognition or no memory of Mr. Welch's recommending either Mr. Fisher or anybody else as counsel for this committee. I will recognize Mr. Welch."

McCarthy pulled himself around, his back to Welch, and in a loud voice ordered James Juliana to get a copy of a news story about Fred Fisher as well as citations that showed he had been linked to the Communist Party, insisting all the while that Welch had recommended Fisher to the committee, that he intended to place this information in the record.

In his book, *Days of Shame,* Senator Charles E. Potter wrote of this incident: "Once again, McCarthy was lying as he had time and again through the hearings. Welch had never recommended Fisher to assist him."

Now Joseph Welch, voice charged with emotion, answered Joe McCarthy directly: "You won't need anything in the record when I have finished telling you this.

"Until this moment, Senator, I think I never really gauged your cruelty or your recklessness. Fred Fisher is a young man who went to the Harvard Law School and came into my firm and is starting what looks to be a brilliant career with me.

"When I decided to work for this committee, I asked Jim St. Clair, who sits on my right, to be my first assistant. I said to Jim, 'Pick somebody in the firm who works under you that you would like.' He chose Fred Fisher, and they came down on an afternoon plane. That night, when we had taken a little stab at trying to see what the case was about, Fred Fisher and Jim St. Clair and I went to dinner together. I then said to these two young men, 'Boys, I don't know anything about you except I have always liked you, but if there is anything funny in the life of either one of you that would hurt anybody in this case, you speak up quick.'

"Fred Fisher said, 'Mr. Welch, when I was in law school and for a period of months after, I belonged to the Lawyers' Guild. . . . I am secretary of the Young Republicans' League in Newton with the son of the Massachusetts governor, and I have the respect and admiration of my community, and I am sure I have the respect and admiration of the twenty-five lawyers or so in Hale and Dorr' [the Welch law firm in Boston].

"I said, 'Fred, I just don't think I am going to ask you to work on the case. If I do, one of these days that will come out and go over national television, and it will just hurt like the dickens.'

"So, Senator, I asked him to go back to Boston. Little did I dream you could be so reckless and so cruel as to do an injury to that lad. It is true that he is still with Hale and Dorr. It is true that he will continue to be with Hale and Dorr. It is, I regret to say, equally true that I fear he shall always bear a scar needlessly inflicted by you. If it were in my power to forgive you for your reckless cruelty, I would do so. I'd like to think I am a gentleman, but your forgiveness will have to come from someone other than me."

McCarthy listened, glaring at Welch from under bunched brows, tongue working over his lips, drawn tight, seemingly determined to strip away the final veneer of propriety, to reveal his essential self to the watching nation. Like a prizefighter bloodied and benumbed, he struck out wildly.

"May I say that Mr. Welch talks about this being cruel and reckless. He was just baiting; he had been baiting Mr. Cohn here for hours, requesting that Mr. Cohn, before sundown, get out of any department of government anyone who is serving the Communist cause. I just gave this man's record, and I want to say, Mr. Welch, that it has been labeled long before he became a member, as early as 1944—"

Welch cut through the torrent of words. "Senator, may we not drop this? We know he belonged to the Lawyers' Guild, and Mr. Cohn nods his head at me. I did you, I think, no personal injury, Mr. Cohn?"

"No, sir," Cohn said quietly.

"I meant to do you no personal injury, and if I did, I beg your pardon. Let us not assassinate this lad [Fisher] further, Senator. You have done enough. Have you no sense of decency, sir, at long last? Have you left no sense of decency?"

With Roy Cohn shaking his head negatively in McCarthy's direction, with Chairman Mundt trying to terminate the exchange, the Senator from Wisconsin was unable to stop what he had begun.

"I would like to finish this," he mumbled. All the talk of

decency and character assassination was apparently beyond his comprehension. Fairness, the right, legal way of doing things, had never much concerned him. The technique of innuendo and allegation, of guilt presumed and exaggerated, of the untruth repeated again and again, had always worked for him, and he saw no reason why it should not work once more. "Mr. Welch," he went on, "has been filibustering this hearing, he has been talking day after day about how he wants to get anyone tainted with Communism out before sundown. I know Mr. Cohn would rather not have me go into this. I intend to, however. Mr. Welch talks about any sense of decency. If I say anything which is not the truth, then I would like to know about it."

At that point, McCarthy read a description of the Lawyers' Guild, then repeated his charge that Welch had recommended Fred Fisher to the committee, ignoring the denials, ignoring the facts.

"It seems," McCarthy continued, "that Mr. Welch is pained so deeply he thinks it is improper for me to give the record, the Communist-front record, of the man whom he wanted to foist on this committee. But it doesn't pain him at all—there is no pain in his chest about the unfounded charges against Mr. Frank Carr. There is no pain there about the attempts to destroy the reputations and take the jobs away from the young men who were working on my committee.

"And, Mr. Welch, if I have said anything here which is untrue, then tell me. I have heard you and everyone else talk so much about laying the truth upon the table that when I hear—and it is completely phony, Mr. Welch, I have listened to you for a long time—when you say now, before sundown, you must get these people out of government, I want to have it very clear, very clear that you were not so serious about that when you tried to recommend this man for this committee.

"And may I say, Mr. Welch, in fairness to you, I have reason to believe that you did not know about his Communist-front record at the time you recommended him. I don't think you would have recommended him to the committee if you knew that. I think it is entirely possible you learned that after you recommended him."

Senator Mundt felt impelled to correct the impression McCarthy was trying to leave. "The chair would like to say again that he does not believe that Mr. Welch recommended Mr. Fisher as counsel for this committee, because he has, through his office, all the recommendations that were made. He does not recall any that came from Mr. Welch and that would include Mr. Fisher."

McCarthy could not stop. "Mr. Welch, . . . you brought him down, did you not, to act as your assistant?"

A wintry disdain coated Lawyer Welch's voice when he spoke: "Mr. McCarthy, I will not discuss this with you further. You have sat within six feet of me and could have asked me about Fred Fisher. You have brought it out. If there is a God in Heaven, it will do neither you nor your cause any good. I will not discuss it further. I will not ask Mr. Cohn any more questions. You, Mr. Chairman, may, if you will, call the next witness."

The Caucus Room exploded into sound, a roar of approving applause. Chairman Mundt announced a recess.

Joe McCarthy spread his hands, gazed bewilderedly around, asked helplessly, "What did I do?"

Able to ask, he was unable to understand.

XVII

AN END OF A BEGINNING

THE ARMY-MCCARTHY HEARINGS ENDED ON JUNE 17. ON THE last day of August, the Special Committee issued a report. Four reports, actually. Two of the Republican members claimed the Army had not proved its charges, although Roy Cohn had been "unduly persistent and aggressive" in behalf of David Schine. The Democratic members believed that McCarthy and Cohn had behaved improperly. Senator Potter, a Republican, said that the Army's charges were "borne out" and that there "may have been subornation or perjury." Senator Everett Dirksen, also a Republican, failed to perceive any wrongdoing on the part of McCarthy or his aides.

For all the time spent, all the evidence, the many witnesses, the contentions back and forth, the hearings had proved nothing conclusive—neither to the Senators nor to the American people. Yet large numbers of citizens were startled and repelled by what had occurred, shamed and disgusted, and serious questions were being asked about Senator McCarthy, his methods and his behavior.

Senator Ralph Flanders introduced a resolution of censure against McCarthy, calling attention to his contempt of the Senate, his contempt for truth, his "habitual contempt for people." The resolution ended:

> RESOLVED, that the conduct of the Senator from Wisconsin, Mr. McCarthy, is unbecoming a member of the United States Senate, is contrary to Senatorial traditions, and tends to bring the Senate into disrepute.

Now the Senate, in its wisdom, had to consider that resolution, which meant another committee was needed to study Senator McCarthy's official behavior. Vice President Richard Nixon announced that six Senators were to compose a Select Committee for that purpose, with Senator Arthur V. Watkins, Republican of Utah, as chairman. Two other Republicans on the committee were Francis Case of South Dakota and Frank Carlson of Kansas. The three Democrat Senators were Samuel Erwin, Jr., of North Carolina, Edwin C. Johnson of Colorado and John C. Stennis of Mississippi.

The Select Committee directed its attention to the Army-McCarthy Hearings, as well as all the other verbal excesses and activities of Joe McCarthy. There were, for example, the false or misleading accusations he had leveled against various individuals, frequently the result of sloppy work by him and his staff. There was McCarthy's failure to recognize the danger that lay in accepting as fact every rumor and baseless charge made by informants who might very well have been motivated by their own prejudices, personal or otherwise. There were the often unjustified attacks made by McCarthy from behind the barricade of Senatorial immunity, his attempt to do damage to General

George C. Marshall, his role, along with that of Roy Cohn, in heaping abuse on the United States Army and its Secretary. There was his acceptance of a ten thousand dollar fee from the Lustron Corporation, a builder of prefabricated houses, while McCarthy was a member of the Senate Banking Committee and a member of a Joint House-Senate Committee on Housing.

And further, there was McCarthy's wild threat to subpoena President Truman before his committee. Also, his attempts to intimidate reporters who were critical of his activities, imputing Communist leanings to newspapers whose policies displeased him. There were, too, the crude attacks he had made against other Senators, the repeated release of classified security information in defiance of the law, his insistence on labeling people and institutions as Communist when they opposed him. And there were still more charges against him.

All charges were considered objectively and with a minimum of passion as Chairman Watkins made every effort to keep the proceedings out of the headlines. When its deliberations were completed, the Select Committee recommended that the Senate censure Joe McCarthy on two counts:

First, his conduct toward the Senate Subcommittee on Privileges and Elections had been "contemptuous, contumacious, and denunciatory, without reason or justification, and was obstructive to the legislative processes. . . ."

Second, McCarthy's abuse of General Ralph Zwicker was held to have been "reprehensible."

But when the Senate as a whole got around to voting on the issue, they considered an amended version of the Select Committee's resolution. The matter of General Zwicker was dropped, it being held that the general had provoked Senator McCarthy sufficiently to warrant his extreme reaction.

Instead, the Senate substituted abuse by McCarthy of the Select Committee. McCarthy had accused the Select Committee of being a "lynch party" and its chairman, Senator Watkins, of "the most unusual, the most cowardly thing I've heard of." He had also characterized the committee as the "unwitting handmaiden," "involuntary agent" and "attorneys in fact" of the Communist Party.

On December 2, the Senate finally took action. It voted 67 to 22 to "condemn" Joe McCarthy, using that term in place of "censure." He was the fourth Senator to be so rebuked by his colleagues.

Because of the Army-McCarthy Hearings under the unyielding eye of the television cameras, because of the heavy press coverage, because of the Senate's condemnation, millions of Americans came to understand now for the first time that Joe McCarthy was in fact a destructive and dangerous force, a dissenter from Constitutional guarantees, a demagogue, the true enemy of justice and freedom, of law and order.

McCarthy had been delivered a crucial blow. Yet at first neither he nor his followers understood what had taken place. He had retained much of his popularity, his adherents being convinced still that he was a victim of the very forces that he had so loudly and aggressively been opposing. Roy Cohn, who had returned to the world of big law and big business, expressed the sentiments of many in the McCarthy camp: "Joe McCarthy and I would rather have American people of this type than all the politicians in the world."

McCarthy, so deeply a politician, may have disagreed. For no longer was he the most important member of the most exclusive club in the world, as the United States Senate has been termed. His status had diminished and his power was gone—also his ability to intimidate his colleagues. He continued to voice threats but the implicit danger that had been couched in the term "McCarthyism" no longer frightened other Senators.

Nor was McCarthy able to exert any influence on the Executive Branch. He was seldom invited to important receptions and dinners and cocktail parties; his nominee for a postmastership was rejected; and when he tried to stop the appointment of Paul Hoffman to the United Nations General Assembly, he was ignored.

McCarthy had been effectively pushed out of the limelight. Roy Cohn had left him, David Schine had slipped back into the obscurity from which he had come, the functionaries had disappeared and the press paid no particular attention to him.

McCarthy failed to attend the Republican National Convention in 1956 and played almost no part in the elections that year. Much of the energy and spirit that had marked him seemed to have evaporated, and it became evident that he was a sick man. He lost more than forty pounds in a few weeks. He suffered from a herniated diaphragm and was in frequent pain.

Always a heavy drinker, he drank more than ever in those days, though this did not mean he became blatantly drunk. Toward the end of April, 1957, he entered the Naval Medical Center at Bethesda, Maryland, supposedly for treatment of a "knee injury." Around Washington, it was assumed he was being "dried out" after a drinking bout. But this time it was neither the knee nor alcohol. At two minutes after 6 P.M. on May 2, 1957, Joe McCarthy died of what was called "acute hepatitic infection."

The man was gone but McCarthyism lived on. McCarthy had held up a mirror and shown America its ugly side, a side that denied to many of its own people the freedom and justice of which it boasted. McCarthy thrived on the fear and apprehension of a generation made weary by a long war, by the loss to Communism of China, by the ghost of a Great Depression. It was a generation that craved a better way of life and found it in rising expectations with the close of World War II, only to see that life threatened by the Soviet Union abroad and challenged by the upward thrust of the poor and deprived minorities at home. For many Americans, it became easy to couple the two under a single heading, viewing the legitimate aspirations of millions of people around the world as something evil and subversive.

As a result, instead of dealing constructively with problems at home and overseas, America found itself diverted by wild and undocumented charges. McCarthy turned up no spies, no foreign agents, and only widened the gulf between Americans of differing opinions, making the struggle against Communism that much more difficult.

McCarthy required the dark shadow of Communism in order to thrive, and he nourished that specter to satisfy his own greed for power and prestige. He made no attempt to adjudicate his differences with other men, no attempt to locate the solid ground that existed between extreme positions. He was concerned only with promoting the rightness of what he said and did. Those who would have denied him this privilege were labeled "evil" or "treasonous" or "phony," their motives suspect. Only McCarthy and his friends were pure of purpose. Only they were patriots. Only they were honest and above suspicion.

President Eisenhower wrote that "un-American activity cannot be prevented or routed out by employing un-American methods; to preserve freedom we must use the tools that freedom provides."

In the end, the man McCarthy was less important than McCarthyism, that reckless and self-righteous assault designed to blacken reputations without due process, to destroy orderly procedure, to insinuate wrongdoing and duplicity where neither existed.

Patriotism, sincerity, truth have never been the province of any one group nor the manifestations of any particular point of view. Nor is character assassination a singular effort, done by the assassin alone. The act requires tacit or active encouragement by those who approve of and enjoy such excesses. Inevitably, once unloosed, forces of this nature leap the tracks of their stated aims and run amok, taking on a terrible existence of their own.

If, out of fear and reaction, men may be destroyed politically, socially, economically, they may also be physically destroyed should they raise their heads above the crowd. Such men become targets for those who are bitter, disaffected, alienated from the mainstream of life. John F. Kennedy became such a target. And Martin Luther King. Malcolm X. Robert F. Kennedy. The end of violence, verbal or otherwise, is always more violence.

McCarthy and McCarthyism were an unsettling reminder to America that under law men are innocent until proved guilty. That an untruth told and retold does not constitute evidence. That to accuse is not to convict. That a public forum is no trial by jury.

McCarthyism was a war against freedom. A battle was won, but the war goes on. And vigilance in defense of liberty has always been in order.

BIBLIOGRAPHY

Anderson, Jack, and May, Ronald W., *McCarthy, the Man, the Senator, the "Ism."* Boston, Beacon Press, 1952.
Barth, Alan, *The Loyalty of Free Men.* New York, Viking Press, 1950.
Bernstein, Barton J., and Matusow, Allen J. (eds.), *The Truman Administration.* New York, Harper & Row, Inc., 1966.
Buckley, William F., Jr., and Bozell, L. Brent, *McCarthy and His Enemies.* Chicago, Henry Regnery Company, 1954.
Cohn, Roy, *McCarthy.* New York, New American Library, 1968.
Donovan, Robert J., *Eisenhower: The Inside Story.* New York, Harper & Bros., 1956.
Eisenhower, President Dwight D., *Mandate For Change.* Garden City, N. Y., Doubleday & Company, Inc., 1963.
Goldman, Eric F., *The Crucial Decade.* New York, Alfred A. Knopf, Inc., 1956.
Gore, Leroy, *Joe Must Go.* New York, Julian Messner, Inc., 1954.
Hart, Hornell Norris, "McCarthy Versus the State Department; toward consensus on certain charges against the State Department by Senator Joseph R. McCarthy and Others. An impartial factual analysis," rev. ed., Durham, N. C., 1952.
Lattimore, Owen, *Ordeal by Slander.* Boston, Little, Brown and Co., 1950.
Lokos, Lionel, *Who Promoted Peress?* New York, Bookmailer, 1961.
McCarthy, Senator Joseph R., *McCarthyism, the Fight for America.* New York, Devin-Adair, 1952.

BIBLIOGRAPHY

Phillips, Cabell, *The Truman Presidency*. New York, The Macmillan Company, 1966.

Potter, Senator Charles E., *Days of Shame*. New York, Coward-McCann, Inc., 1965.

Rorty, James and Decter, Moshe, *McCarthy and the Communists*. Boston, The Beacon Press, 1954.

Rovere, Richard H., *Senator Joe McCarthy*. Cleveland, The World Publishing Company, 1959.

Sargent, Winthrop, "The Art of Vituperation." *Life* Magazine, October 23, 1950.

Straight, Michael, *Trial by Television*. Boston, The Beacon Press, 1954.

Taylor, Telford, *Grand Inquest*. New York, Simon and Schuster, Inc., 1955.

Truman, President Harry S, *1946-1952: Years of Trial and Hope*. Garden City, N. Y., Doubleday & Co., Inc., 1956.

U. S. Senate, major speeches delivered, 1950-51. Washington, D. C., Government Printing Office, 1953.

U. S. Senate, Committee on Rules and Administration. Investigations of Senators Joseph R. McCarthy and William Benton pursuant to S. Res. 187 and S. Res. 304; report of the Subcommittee on Privileges and Elections to the Committee on Rules and Administration. Washington, D. C., Government Printing Office, 1952. (Boston, Beacon Press, 1953.)

U. S. Senate, Select Committee to Study Censure Charges. Report of the Select Committee to Study Censure Charges, United States Senate, Eighty-third Congress, second session, pursuant to the order on S. Res. 301 and amendments, a resolution to censure the Senator from Wisconsin, Mr. McCarthy. Washington, D. C., Government Printing Office, 1954.

Wisconsin Citizens' Committee on McCarthy's Record. *The McCarthy Record*. Madison, Wisconsin, 1952.

INDEX

Acheson, Dean, 39, 40, 48, 50, 71-2, 76, 91, 96
Adams, John, 123, 130, 151-52, 153, 157
Adams, Sherman, 152, 153
Aiken, George, 66
Amerasia, 13
American Legion, 37
Armed Services Committee (Senate), 84-85
Army Loyalty and Security Appeal Board, 152, 153, 154
Army-McCarthy Hearings, 131, 134-177, 178, 180
Aumer, Hermann, 115
Austin, Warren, 75

Baruch, Bernard, 33
Bentley, Elizabeth, 13, 36, 47
Benton, William, 93, 104, 106
Black, Hugo, 122-23
blacklist, 38, 103
Blaik, Earl, 95
Bradley, Colonel Jack, 146
Brewster, Owen, 86
Britain, British, 32, 41, 50
Browder, Earl, 61, 84
Brownell, Herbert, 152
Buckley, William F., Jr., 50, 101
Budenz, Louis, 61
Butler, Hugh, 40
Butler, John Marshall, 83, 85-86
Byrd, Harry F., 20
Byrnes, James, 24, 45

California Un-American Activities Committee, 55, 56
Camp Kilmer, 120, 121
Canadian spy ring, 23
Capital Times (Madison, Wisc.), 18
Carlson, Frank, 178
Carnegie Endowment for International Peace (Carnegie Foundation), 37
Carr, Francis, 134, 142, 146, 152, 155, 157, 160, 162
Case, Francis, 178
Catholics, Catholicism, 20, 41, 44, 61
Central Intelligence Agency (CIA), 113
Chambers, Whittaker, 13, 36, 37, 47
Chiang Kai-shek, 13, 34, 39, 59, 63-64, 70, 81, 94
China, Chinese, 23, 32, 34, 39, 70, 73, 80, 89, 90, 91, 94, 97, 127, 163, 181
China Lobby, 63-4
China Monthly, 63
Chongchon River, 89
Chou En-lai, 80
Churchill, Winston, 13, 24, 70; Iron Curtain speech, 24
CIA (*see* Central Intelligence Agency)
Clifford, Clark, 21
Coe, Frank, 105
Cohn, Roy, 46, 112-13, 113-16, 127-28, 129, 130, 135, 136, 137, 140, 141, 142, 145-46, 147, 148-49,

187

INDEX

151-52, 155, 157, 158, 161, 162, 164, 165-69, 171, 173, 177, 179, 180, 181; European tour, 113-16
Cold War, 33
Coleman, Thomas, 15
Commonweal, 87
Communism, Communists, 12, 13, 18, 23, 27, 29, 31-32, 33, 34, 36, 37, 38, 39, 40, 41, 44-45, 47, 48, 49, 50, 51, 52, 54-57, 61, 62, 74, 83, 87, 90, 91, 92, 93, 104, 106, 107, 109, 111, 112, 116, 122-23, 124, 128-29, 134, 138, 142, 155, 162, 163, 164, 167, 169, 170, 171, 173, 174, 179, 182
Connors, Bradley, 69-70
conservatism, 13, 19, 30, 32, 41
Coplon, Judith, 38
Crouch, Paul, 155
Czechoslovakia, 23, 35

Daily Worker (Communist), 61, 103, 104
Davis, Elmer, 94
Democrats, 18, 32, 35, 44, 65, 67, 102, 105
DeSola, Ralph, 92
Dewey, Thomas E., 35, 36
Dien Bien Phu, 133
Dies Committee, 14
Dies, Martin, 14
Dirksen, Everett McKinley, 134, 177
Dixiecrat Party, 35
Dodd, Dr. Bella, 61
Driscoll, Mrs. Mary Brinkley, 158-60
Dulles, John Foster, 75, 109-110, 111
Dworshak, Henry, 134

economy, black market, 22, 29; inflation, 22, 95; postwar, 19-20, 25, 29, 38-9, 40
Einstein, Albert, 117
Eisenhower, Dwight David, 105, 106, 107, 109, 110, 111, 116-17, 153, 155, 182
Eisler, Gerhart, 115
Erwin, Samuel, Jr., 178
espionage, 13-14, 29, 38, 45, 47, 59, 61, 128-29, 163, 165-67, 169, 182
Executive Branch, 111, 153, 154, 156, 164, 181

Far Eastern strategy, 71, 76
FBI (*see* Federal Bureau of Investigation)
Fedder, William, 85-86
Federal Bureau of Investigation (FBI), 13, 27, 28, 38, 45, 54, 57, 60-61, 65, 93, 142-43, 154, 155, 167
Field, Frederick Vanderbilt, 61-62
Finland, 35, 62
Fisher, Fred, 170-175
Flanagan, Francis D., 112
Flanders, Ralph, 124, 160, 178
foreign aid, 71
foreign policy, 22, 94, 100, 109, 110
Formosa, 39, 74, 81. *See also* Nationalist China
Fort Dix, 129-30, 140
Fort Monmouth, 128, 141, 165-67, 168
France, French, 23, 74, 133
Freedman, Benjamin, 92
Fuchs, Klaus, 38, 46

Germans, Germany, 22, 32, 34
Gillette, Guy M., 104
Gold, Harry, 38
Goodwin, William J., 63
Greece, 32-33
Greenglass, David, 38

Hale and Dorr, 172, 173
Harding, Warren G., 12
Harris, William, 92
Harvard University, 93

188

INDEX

Hatch Act, 28
Heil, Julius P., 15-16
Hemingway, Ernest, 56
Hendrickson, Robert, 66
Hensel, H. Struve, 152
Hickenlooper, Bourke, 54
Hiss, Alger, 36, 37, 40, 46, 47, 57, 105
Ho Chi Minh, 133-34
Hoffman, Paul, 181
Hoover, Herbert, 95
Hoover, J. Edgar, 57, 60-61, 65, 142, 157
House Committee on Un-American Activities, 14, 37, 55, 56, 107

Indochina, 74, 133
inflation (see economy)
Institute for Pacific Relations, 59
Internal Security Committee (see House Committee on Un-American Activities)
Isaacs, Hon. Stanley, 56
isolationism, 22, 23
Italy, 23, 33, 35
Ives, Irving, 66

Jackson, Henry, 134, 139
Jaffe, Philip, 13
Japan, 11, 20, 32, 34, 70, 74, 77, 98
Jenkins, Ray H., 135, 138, 139, 140, 142, 145, 146, 147, 148, 158, 161, 162, 165
Jenner, William, 50, 107
Jessup, Professor Philip Caryl, 63
Jews, 20, 25, 40, 91, 92
Johnson, Alvanley, 21
Johnson, Edwin C., 178
Johnson, Hewlett, 56
Johnson, Louis A., 75
Joint Chiefs of Staff, 71, 80, 94, 96, 99, 100, 110
Jonkel, Jon, 86
Juliana, James, 147, 148, 171

Kaghan, Theodore, 116, 138
Kaltenborn, H. V., 36
Kefauver, Estes, 96
Kennan, George, 34
Kennedy, John F., 183
Kennedy, Robert F., 112, 183
Kent, Carleton, 157
Kenyon, Judge Dorothy, 55
Kerr, Jean, 83
King, Martin Luther, 183
Kohlberg, Alfred, 63, 86
Korea, 32, 64, 69-74, 80, 82, 84, 85, 91, 95, 96, 105, 107, 108, 127; North Korea, 70, 71, 72, 73, 79, 108; South Korea (Republic of), 64, 69, 70, 71, 73, 75, 76, 77, 80, 89, 94, 96, 108; truce, 108
Kraus, Charles H., 43, 44, 45
Ku Klux Klan, 37

labor, organized, 20, 40
La Follette, Robert M., Jr., 16, 17, 18
Larsen, Emanuel, 13
Lattimore, Owen J., 59, 60, 61, 62, 64-65, 93, 112
Lawyers' Guild, 172, 173, 174
Lehman, Herbert H., 53, 93
Lewis, Fulton, Jr., 63, 92
Lewis, John L., 20
Lie, Trygve, 72
Lodge, Henry Cabot, Jr., 54, 152
loyalty program, 19, 27-28, 37, 54, 102
Loyalty Review Board, 28, 54
Lucas, Scott, 20, 51, 52
Lustron Corporation, 179
Lyons, Eugene, 62

MacArthur, General Douglas, 62, 69, 73, 75, 76-77, 79, 80, 81, 82-83, 89, 90, 94, 96, 97, 98, 99, 100, 105
McCarthy, Bridget Tierney (mother), 8

INDEX

McCarthy Committee, 111, 112, 113, 121, 122, 128, 130, 153, 155, 157, 164
McCarthy, Joseph Raymond, early years and education, 7-9; first politics, 8-9; circuit judge, 9; Marine Corps, 7, 9, 10; Tail Gunner Joe, 15-17; campaigns against La Follette, 16-18; first actions in Congress, 30-32; the Colony dinner, 43-44; selects Communism as his issue, 43-46; begins lecturing, 47; Valentine interview, 48-49; claims Communists in State Department, 49-53; Tydings Committee hearings, 53-67; committee report, 83; charges Judge Kenyon, 55-56; names Lattimore top spy, 59-63; China Lobby support, 63-64; Republican Declaration of Conscience, 66-67; defeats Tydings' election, 83-87; attacks Anna Rosenberg, 91-93; accusations and unsupported allegations, 91-94; 100, 103; degrades General Marshall, 100-102; Senator Benton attempts censure, 104-105; campaigns for Eisenhower; defeats Benton's reelection, 105-107; McCarthy Committee formed, 111-12; sends Cohn and Schine on European tour, 113-17; examines Peress, 121-23; examines General Zwicker, 124-26; tries to get commission for Schine, 127-28; Army demands hearing, 130-31; Army-McCarthy Hearings, 134-75; persecutes General Reber, 136-40; humiliates Secretary of Army Stevens, 140-42; exhibits doctored picture, 145-48; subpoenas Loyalty Board members; President intervenes, 152-55; declares himself above Executive power, 154-56; strange memoranda, 157-60; implicates Fred Fisher, 169-75; Senate censure, 178-80; death, 181.
McCarthy, Mrs. Joseph R. (see Kerr, Jean)
McCarthy, Timothy (father), 8
McClellan, John, 134, 135, 138-39, 143, 155, 156-57
McLeod, Scott, 111
McMahon, Brien, 56
MacLeish, Archibald, 105
Magraw, James, 92
Malcolm X., 183
Malenkov, Georgi, 108
Mao Tse-tung, 23, 34, 39
Marshall, George C., 31, 32, 33, 34, 39, 64, 96, 101-2, 104, 179
Marshall Plan, 35, 40, 62
Martin, Joseph W., 97
Massing, Hede, 115
Miller, Ruth McCormick, 83, 86
mines (soft-coal) strike, 20
Morris, Robert, 83
Morse, Wayne, 64, 66
Mundt, Karl, 134-35, 139, 142, 143, 156, 161, 169, 171, 173, 175
Mundy, Cornelius, 83, 84

National Council of Soviet-American Friendship, 55, 56
Nationalist China, 63, 64. See also Formosa
NATO (see North Atlantic Treaty Organization)
Negroes, 20, 25, 32, 35, 40, 81, 91
Nellor, Edward, 92
New Deal, 12, 13, 32, 37, 40, 41, 45, 53
New York Times, 135
Nixon, Richard M., 50, 105, 178
North Atlantic Treaty Organization (NATO), 91

Pearson, Drew, 93
Pegler, Westbrook, 63

INDEX

Peress, Dr. Irving, 119-124, 125
Philippines, The, 74
photographs, doctored, 84, 145-47
Plain-Dealer (Cleveland, Ohio), 81-82
Poland, 22
Policy Planning Staff (PPS), 34
Potter, Charles E., 134, 136, 171-72, 177
Price, Sergeant John, 81
Progressive Party, 35
Pusey, Nathan, 93

railroads, 20, 21, 95
Ramparts, 113
Reber, Maj. Gen. Miles, 127, 136-39
Reber, Sam, 137-40
Reconstruction Finance Corporation, 95
Red Channels, 38, 103
Republican Declaration of Conscience, 66-67
Republicans, 15, 16, 17, 25, 27, 32, 35, 37, 47, 62, 65, 66-67, 91, 102, 106, 108, 109, 110
Rhee, Syngman, 71, 72, 85
Richardson, Seth B., 28
Ridgway, General Matthew, 110
Roberts, William A., 44, 45
Robinson, Jackie, 29
Rogers, William, 152
Roosevelt, Franklin D., 12, 24, 40, 70
Rosenberg, Mrs. Anna, 91, 92-93
Rosenberg, Ethel, 38, 108, 112
Rosenberg, Julius, 38, 108, 112
Roth, Lt. Andrew, 13
Rusk, Dean, 80, 96
Russia, Russians (*see* Soviet Union)

Sabath, Adolph, 46
St. Clair, James, 171-72
Schine, G. David, 112-13, 113-16, 127-30, 134, 136, 137, 138, 140-41, 145-46, 147-48, 152, 155, 160, 164, 165, 177, 181; European tour, 113-16
Select (Censure) Committee, 178-80
Seoul (So. Korea), 69, 75
Service, John Stewart, 13, 47
Smith, Frank M., 84
Smith, Gerald L. K., 92
Smith, Margaret Chase, 66-67
Sokolsky, George, 63, 113
South America, 23
Soviet Union, 19, 23, 24, 29, 32, 34, 35, 38, 62, 64, 70, 71, 72-73, 75, 80, 94, 108, 127, 163, 182
Spellman, Francis Cardinal, 41
spies (*see* espionage)
sports scandals, 95
Stalin, Joseph, 34, 70, 108
State Department, 46, 47, 48, 49, 50, 51, 52, 57, 60, 69, 90, 104, 105, 111, 116, 117
State Journal (Wisconsin), 17
Stennis, John C., 178
Stevens, Robert, 128, 129, 130, 140-42, 145-46, 147, 152, 157, 161, 167-69, 179
Stevenson, Adlai E., 105, 110
Sun-Times (Chicago, Ill.), 157
Supreme Court, 14
Surine, Don, 86, 92
Swift, Rev. Wesley, 91-92
Symington, Stuart, 134, 147

Taft-Hartley Act, 32
Taft, Robert A., 22, 30, 31, 35, 62, 75, 95, 102, 103-4, 107, 111
Taiwan (*see* Formosa)
thirty-eighth parallel, 70, 73, 80, 90, 96, 97, 108
Thomas, Parnell, 50
Thorpe, Brig. Gen. Elliot, 62
Thurmond, Strom, 35
Thye, Edward, 66

INDEX

Times-Herald (Washington, D.C.), 63, 83, 84
Tobey, Charles, 66
Tribune (Chicago, Ill.), 36, 40-41, 63
Truman Doctrine, 33, 34
Truman, Harry S., 11, 14, 21, 24, 25, 27, 33, 35, 36, 37, 39, 40, 46, 49, 50, 57, 60, 62, 71, 72, 73, 75, 76, 77, 80, 81, 82, 90, 91, 94, 95, 96, 97, 98, 99, 101, 104, 105, 108, 115, 179
Turkey, 33
Tydings Committee, 60-62, 64, 65, 83
Tydings, Millard, 53, 54, 56, 57, 65, 83, 84, 86, 87, 147

Un-American Activities Committee (*see* House Committee on Un-American Activities)
United Nations, 23, 24, 37, 40, 51, 71, 72, 73, 74, 76, 79, 80, 90, 91, 94, 96, 97
United States Army, 70, 75, 77, 79, 81, 82, 110, 124-26, 129-31, 162, 179
Urey, Dr. Harold, 56
Utley, Freda, 62

Valentine, Dan, 48-49
Vandenberg, Arthur H., 22-23
Velde, Harold, 107
Vietminh, 133
Voice of America, 52, 113

Wadleigh, Julian, 47
Wallace, Henry, 24, 25, 35, 59
Walsh, Father Edmund A., 44, 45
Warren, Earl, 133
Watkins, Arthur V., 178, 179, 180
Welch, Joseph, 137, 139, 142, 143-44, 146, 147-48, 158-60, 161, 165-69, 170-75
West Point Academy, 95
White, Harry Dexter, 14
White, Lincoln, 49
Whitney, Alexander, 21
Wicker, Irene, 103
Wiley, Alexander, 9
Willoughby, Gen. Charles A., 80
Wilson, Charles, 153, 154
Wilson, Woodrow, 12

Yalta (Agreement), 19
Yugoslavia, 75

Zwicker, Brig. Gen. Ralph W., 121, 124-26, 179